THE CHANGING FACE OF Grantham

THE CHANGING FACE OF Grantham

in association with the Grantham Journal

Journal

First published in Great Britain in 2004 by

The Breedon Books Publishing Company Limited

Breedon House, 3 The Parker Centre,

Derby, DE21 4SZ.

ISBN 1 85983 431 0

Printed and bound by Butler & Tanner,

Frome, Somerset, England.

Cover printing by Lawrence-Allen Colour Printers,

Weston-super-Mare, Somerset, England.

Contents

Foreword

FOR 150 years the *Grantham Journal* has reflected in its news columns and advertisements the changing face of the town it has been proud to serve.

Grantham can trace its roots from the Bronze Age and the town we would recognise today began to take shape after the Norman Conquest with the building of St Wulfram's Church, the Angel Hotel and later the King's School where Sir Isaac Newton was famously educated.

Many of the best buildings were erected during the Georgian period and old photographs show a handsome, charming town built around the wide carriageway of the Old North Road.

It was the industrial revolution and the arrival of the railways that dramatically altered Grantham. The sleepy market community was galvanised by the construction in 1852 of the first railway station, 100 miles from London and the perfect distance to change steam engines on the route north. By this stage Richard Hornsby's iron works were producing 14 engines at any one time and more than 500 men were employed in 'Hell's Kitchen'.

In February 1854 the *Grantham Journal of Useful, Instructive and Entertaining Knowledge and Monthly Advertiser* went on sale at one penny. The first issue coincided with the State Opening of Parliament by Queen Victoria and much of the front page was devoted to her speech. But it did feature some local advertisements and railway timetables and the newspaper became a success, quickly switching to weekly publication.

As technology improved (and the number of pages in its newspaper increased) so Grantham advanced to become the thriving industrial town many of today's older residents still recall fondly. Aveland Barford arrived in 1933, cutting the jobless figure from 2,350 to 1,600, while other big players such as R.H. Neal and BMARC followed.

World War Two had a dramatic effect on Grantham, as it became the most bombed town of its size, attracting the Luftwaffe through its strategically important rail links but mainly the factories producing shells, bullets and guns.

In 1945 Alfred Roberts became Mayor, his daughter Margaret having been head girl at Kesteven and Grantham Girls' School two years previously. She went on to Oxford University and of course, as Margaret Thatcher, became Britain's first woman Prime Minister. She rarely returned to her hometown.

After the war Grantham prospered, its heavy manufacturing base providing plenty of well-paid employment in the '50s and '60s. But as the large factories ground to a halt, *Journal* headlines began to tell of mass redundancies, intransigent unions, strikes and a realisation that the good times were over.

As the supermarkets and service industries replaced the heavy industry and the factories lay empty, Grantham was left without its market town charm or the industrial energy that had replaced it.

Now it is reinventing itself as a sub-regional shopping centre, salvaging the best of what is left and trying to plan with real purpose.

The *Journal* has reflected all these changes in its 150 years and will continue to do so. It has been my privilege to be one of only 10 editors in that time and I am grateful to my colleagues John Pinchbeck and Gerry Wright for their work in putting together the words and the pictures for this book.

What better way to mark 150 years?

Nick Woodhead
Managing Editor, Grantham Journal

Trade & Industry

Grantham Journal

The *Grantham Journal* was first published in 1854 by Joseph Rogers, a jobbing printer based in Watergate. The newspaper was taken over by the Escritt family in 1862 and four years later moved to its present High Street site. Until then the building was a coaching inn called the Mail Hotel. The archway remained until late 1958 when the frontage was knocked down and incorporated into F.W. Woolworth's new store. Extensions were also built at the rear. The company was bought by EMAP in 1984 and in 1996 was acquired by Johnston Press.

The side of the *Grantham Journal* in 1957, looking into High Street through the archway, which was once used by stagecoaches. The building opposite was occupied by Mr Wallace the dentist.

The *Journal* building as seen from what later became Greenwoods Row car park. Many of the buildings were pulled down or incorporated into Woolworths and a new *Journal* building in 1957.

The High Street reception of the *Grantham Journal* in March 1957.

The old *Journal* buildings in Greenwoods Row were replaced by the new in May 1959. The paper was printed here by hot metal presses until 1973.

The *Journal's* fleet of vans in 1969. Although the Hillmans and Minivans have been replaced, the rear of the *Journal* remains much the same.

Ruston & Hornsby

Founded by Richard Hornsby in 1815, the factory was built in what was then Spittlegate parish. In no time the factory was expanding between the railway line and the River Witham. Originally an agricultural machinery maker, the company created a revolutionary plough which led to ground-breaking (literally) achievements worldwide. It also made steam engines, developed the first compression engine in 1892 and the crawler tractor in the early 1900s. The latter invention led to the military tank being developed at Lincoln. Later Ruston and Hornsby, the company boomed until the 1960s when it was slimmed down and became Alfred Wiseman until its closure. For a spell the old buildings were used as workshops for emerging businesses then were gradually demolished to be replaced by retail outlets for national companies.

Ruston and Hornsby packing department busy stencilling an order for Saudi Arabia in 1954, which amounted to 247 tonnes of equipment worth £70,000 and was sent by rail. It was part of a two-year contract to supply 1,100 oil engines for an irrigation scheme.

The foundry in 1926. This building was on Spring Gardens. Here, patterns were filled with molten metal to create castings.

The heavy machine shop in 1926 where health and safety were of little consideration. Many of the moving parts, including belt drives and gears, were exposed.

Little is known about these cellars running under Ruston and Hornsby's factory which stood on London Road and many myths were created over the years including that they housed skeletons. They were believed to predate the factory, which was begun in 1815. Variously they were used to store wrought iron and office records. They were filled in when the factory was demolished to make way for a retail park.

Demolition men moved into the three-storey house on London Road, next door to the John Lee factory. It was built in Georgian times by industrialist Richard Hornsby, who was so hands-on, he had a door directly into the factory. By 1974 it had been empty for many years.

The final traces of Ruston and Hornsby's empire were to be swept away in 1988. Top End, off North Parade, which included 31 fitting shop and packing shop had been used by Aveling Barford, but was by then surplus to their requirements. It was rebuilt as a builders' merchants and later a trading estate.

Inside the Ruston and Hornsby building on the corner of Station Road and London Road in 1997. Formerly the sales department, these women were working for Bridal Fashions making wedding dresses.

BMARC

ARMS maker BMARC opened for business at a factory on Springfield Road in 1938. It began with 150 jobs but during the war up to 6,000 people were employed there. The general manager was Denis Kendall, a controversial character who became the town's wartime MP and went on to develop cars, motorcycles and tractors, without too much success. In 1971 Swiss company Oerlikon took over and by 1976 over 1,000 people worked there. In the 1980s first Astra then Royal Ordnance took over. It closed in 1993 with the loss of the final 25 jobs.

But BMARC was not just about work – play was high on the agenda. After the demise of Ruston and Hornsby, BMARC encouraged both the town's boxing club and the town band. When rock 'n' roll came to Grantham, the very first session was staged at BMARC Social Club in February 1957. While other clubs had notices saying 'jiving and bopping prohibited', the cool cats at the BMARC club were throwing their young chicks about in a jiving competition. The music was supplied by, among others, the Vagabonds, a group that went on to win second place in a national skiffle competition. The group included Brian Locking, who later played for the Shadows, and Roy Taylor, who became a pop star, and TV presenter Vince Eager.

The new BMARC building under construction in 1979. This administration block cost £1.9 million. Managing director Werner Leuch said the building marked the company's confidence in the future, especially the next 20 years. The company lasted scarcely another 12. The building later became Springfield Conference Centre.

A children's Christmas party in BMARC Social Club in 1953, Coronation year. The bar in the left corner had yet to be built, but the propeller from a Junkers Ju88 shot down by factory gunners still had pride of place on the back wall.

Grantham's first twist competition was in May 1962. Organised by Huntingtower Road Allotment Association, it was staged at BMARC Social Club. Dancing to the Pontiacs, one of the winning couples were 'Nifty' Andrews and Miss J. Mottershaw, who won a camera and travelling clock.

From the same competition, joint winners Miss J. Murphy and Donald Holmes, whose prizes were an electric razor and a hair dryer.

Ken Simmonds at the Wurlitzer organ in BMARC Social Club. Apart from playing a church organ, Ken also played the Compton organ at the Granada cinema.

An £11,000 extension in 1963 made BMARC Social Club one of the most attractive in the county. The club was founded as Beaverbrook Hall early in the war and was opened by newspaper magnate Lord Beaverbrook.

Tiny Smart crosses BMARC swimming pool by pole on the firm's gala day in 1974. Behind it is the sports club where the boxing club trained before moving to its own premises in Alexandra Road.

BMARC workers leave the social club, Springfield Road, after 500 shop floor workers voted to stay on strike.

Aveling Barford

When Aveling Barford moved to Grantham in 1934, the dole queue was slashed from 2,300 to just over 1,000. The road roller manufacturer came from Rochester, Kent, taking the county emblem Invicta as its trade mark. Key personnel were housed in the purpose-built Walton Gardens. After the war, the company became better known for its dumpers and graders. It was taken over by car-maker British Leyland but after they sold in 1978 and following a series of owners, it went into liquidation in 1988 with the loss of 550 jobs. The assets were taken over by Wordsworth Holdings, which found jobs for 300 and retained the former company's name as a trade name.

Prime Minister Sir Alec Douglas Home visited Aveling Barford in 1963. He is seen here inspecting a mechanical shovel.

Road rollers being assembled at Aveling Barford in the 1950s.

Aveling Barford workers coming out of the factory in 1988. The push bike was still a popular form of transport for work but there were fewer employees.

Workmen on bicycles pour out of Aveling Barford in 1971 as the works' siren marks the end of another day. Some 20 years earlier, virtually everyone would have biked to work and at 'going home time' there would be thousands of cyclists on the road.

Striking workmen from Aveling Barford in 1969 outside the factory gates, with the houses of Houghton Road (once Paper Mill Lane) as a backdrop.

Coles Cranes

Cranemaker R.H. Neal came to Grantham in 1937, having bought the former Potters Pump factory, Dysart Road, for £4,000. It specialised in mobile cranes. In 1950 it made the country's biggest mobile crane, which cost £8,000. In the 1960s it was bought by British Crane and Excavator and rebranded Coles Cranes. A booming export market in the 1970s led to a massive expansion but the factory closed in the mid-1980s and at one stage was set to become a national fire museum. The offices eventually became the national headquarters for the Woodland Trust while other units became an industrial estate.

Coles Cranes held an open day at its Dysart Road works in May 1975.

Staff at Coles Cranes walked out after the collapse of pay talks in 1981. The offices were on Dysart Road and were later taken over by the Woodland Trust.

Central TV filming *The Town Mrs Thatcher Left Behind* in 1984. Coles Cranes of Dysart Road is in the background. The company was closed soon afterwards.

Brown Brothers

Brown Brothers went hi-tech in 1954. After supplying milk to their customers for many years from metal churns, and using ladles to fill the housewives' jugs, they installed a bottling plant at their Manthorpe dairy. This may look primitive now, but at the time it was revolutionary.

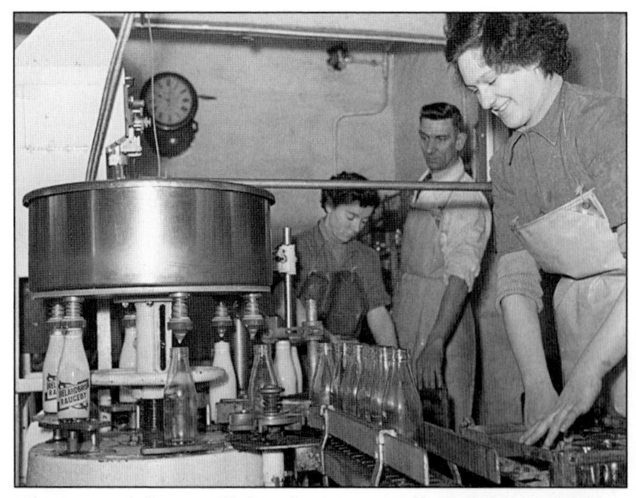

The tops of these milk bottles were cardboard discs which schoolboys used for playing 'milkies', a variation on 'ciggies' played with cigarette cards. On each of Brown Brothers' floats was the slogan: *You may whip our cream but you can't beat our milk.*

Other industry

Grosvenor Furniture, Alma Park (later Quality Furniture) started 1985 with a strike.

T.W. Kempton moved into a new £300,000 factory off Dysart Road in May 1975. It had 22,000sq ft for up to 250 staff. The high-class knitwear firm first arrived in Grantham in 1973.

Work began on Northern Foods' factory, off Swingbridge Road, in 1986, with district council chairman Peter Spiegl and Northern Foods MD John Dicks doing the honours.

Damage put at £50,000 was caused at Vacu-Lug Traction Tyres factory, Gonerby Hill Foot, in July 1954. It took Kesteven Fire Brigade nearly two hours to bring the blaze under control. Between 50 and 60 men were engaged in clearing up but the factory returned to full production within three weeks.

Foundry workers at Caddy Castings arrived one morning to find their factory on fire in September 1980. It was believed to be caused by an electrical fault and damage was put at £100,000. Firemen brought the blaze under control in about 20 minutes. The company produced iron and aluminium castings for the engineering industry.

Pickets from Sheffield descended on Grantham's British Steel depots at Old Wharf Road and Spittlegate Level in support of a 1980 national dispute. They mounted a 24-hour picket. Police were called to help lorries pass over the picket lines. Old Wharf Road was bottled up and Reads canning factory, Springfield Road, was in danger of running out of steel.

Bjorlow tannery closed in 1973 when the owners decided the factory was too antiquated and 180 leatherworkers lost their jobs. The company had developed waterproof suede but despite its innovations, it did not provide the best working conditions in town. The factory was built on what was previously Alexander Shaw's canalside Victorian tannery. The site became Hollis Road industrial estate.

Gas Works

Firefighters tackled a small but difficult blaze at Grantham gasworks in 1955. The gasworks was built in the early 19th century by the side of the Grantham Canal to make coal deliveries easier.

By 1959 the gasworks was redundant as gas was imported from other towns and, later, North Sea gas. From then on, only the gasometers down Gas Works Lane, off Harlaxton Road, remained. This picture shows the last moments of the furnace chimney.

Commerce

Shops

Westmoreland's TV & radio exhibition at the Westgate Hall in September 1958 had the latest in home entertainment. TV personality MacDonald Hobley showed visitors bargains such as a black and white TV for £142 and a radio for a mere £26. To put that into perspective, a labourer would have earned £8 a week.

John Porter and Son's shoe shop began in Elmer Street in 1829. It moved to High Street in 1912 and these larger premises were a few doors away, opened in 1963.

The exterior of John Porter and Son's shoe shop in High Street, opened in 1963. In the window is a display representing the original business in 1829. Porter's were famed locally for impressive window displays.

Arbon's new walkround store at 96 Westgate opened in April 1963. The store began as J.F. Arbon in Watergate in 1923 selling paint, wallpaper and hardware. Ten years later it changed to selling prams before transferring to bigger premises nearby. Over the years they developed into toys and angling equipment and became Arbon and Watts.

An excellent choice of baby carriages and cots in Arbon's new walkround store at 96 Westgate in April 1963. The prams all had sunshades.

Melton Farmers hardware shop was opened by TV personality and Derbyshire farmer Ted Moult in 1963. It was on the site of the Blue Anchor, a small pub which closed in 1961. For many years in the 1980s and 1990s it was Plamore Sport, which closed in 2002. Next door was Geoff Siddaway's motorcycle shop.

Before the nation went hygiene crazy, raw meat was put on display and plucked birds hung from overhead rails. This is the staff of Hammonds' butchers, which was opposite the sorting office, Wharf Road, at Christmas 1961.

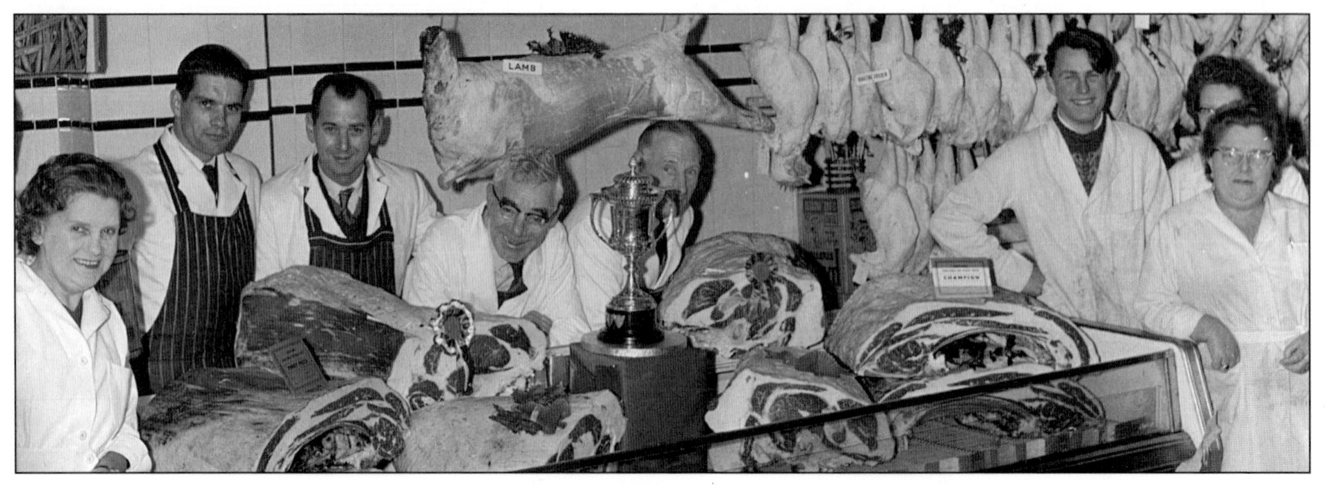

Whipples garage, for many years the town's Vauxhall dealer, finally closed in 1986. The company began as drapers. The premises was taken over by Kwik Fit.

Ask for a 6in by ¼in bolt at this ironmongers and the proprietor would ask for the thread type. If it was ironmongery they stocked it. Owner Ray Tuxworth joined the company as an assistant in 1935 but closed in 1982 unable to find a buyer. He also owned Collards in Westgate, with the distinctive Little Dustpan.

No, gentlemen's outfitter Colin Tipler (centre) didn't bring in a couple of smart new dummies – they are the real thing. Laurel and Hardy came to Grantham in 1952 to open the Chamber of Trade's fair at the Guildhall. The generous pair gave their services for a donation to charity. They also dropped in to Colin's High Street store. In the background is Gladys Foster, wife of the chamber's chairman John Foster. The couple went on to give many years of public service as borough, district and county councillors.

Arthur Chambers, an upmarket dress shop and haberdashers, closed in 1982. Four years later, when this picture was taken, it was beginning to look tatty. In 1987 Yorkshire Bank took it over, converting half into a bank and renting the rest.

Probably the most recognised vehicle in Grantham in the 1950s – Cammack's furniture van. The three main furnishers of the day were Neales, Cammacks and John Hall, although in those days there was room for several smaller businesses. Cammacks occupied the building still home to its namesake in Westgate, which now sells porcelain.

D.E. Chandler's shop showing the latest in kitchens and fireplaces in 1951.

D.E. Chandler's shop in 1951. The doorway was soon filled in to provide more windows. The company claimed it could supply everything from a cotter pin to a combine harvester. To the left is the pub Frederick Fletcher Ltd, later the Market Cross and the Establishment. Star Provisions is on the other side. Chandler's expanded into neighbouring premises in 1987 with its propane gas business.

Pork butchers Watkin & Sons, London Road, closed in 1990 after 78 years. Owner Graham Watkin said he wanted to concentrate on his pub, the Red Lion, Newton.

Smiths Tools, Watergate, in 1990 – Maurice Dove & Peter Green.

Isaac Newton Centre

Grantham's first major shopping development saw many of the town's Victorian buildings fall to the bulldozer. It began before 1980 with demolition of Rutland, Stanton, Bath and Welby streets, together with parts of Wharf Road. The centre, owned by William Morrison, opened in 1984.

Driver Bill Phillips, of Leicester, had a lucky escape when his 35-tonne excavator toppled into the cellar of a Rutland Street house he was demolishing in February 1980. He was making way for the Isaac Newton Shopping Centre. The jib just avoided crashing into the Maltings, which were later developed into a suite of offices.

A steel frame shows the progress of the Isaac Newton Shopping Centre as William Morrison changed the face of Grantham forever. The Greenwoods Row car park was already shrinking in 1983.

The reception area of the Isaac Newton Centre was beginning to take shape in March 1983.

A fashion show inside the Isaac Newton Centre in 1984.

The Isaac Newton Centre was extended in 1997 with a semi-covered mall.

George Centre

The George Centre, built in 1990, was controversially constructed behind the façade of the George Hotel and led to a lot of outbuildings behind coming down. Strangely, this was originally called St Peter's Place but the owners soon found this was confusing as the Isaac Newton Centre was on St Peter's Hill.

Climbing into the tower crane over the George development in 1990 is driver Kenny Robinson.

The George shopping centre begins to take shape in 1990, as seen from a tower crane used during the construction.

ASDA

The opening of the £20 million Asda supermarket with an unprecedented 530 parking spaces in 1998.

Inside the Asda supermarket in August 1998, three months before opening. The 45,000sq ft would make it the biggest supermarket in town.

Trades fairs

Around every three or four years, Grantham Chamber of Trade used to stage a trades fair, where companies showed their wares. This was held at various places, once in the former Ruston and Hornsby factory and several times at the Guildhall, but more often under canvas, including at the London Road sports ground and Greenwoods Row car park.

Grantham Trades Fair was held on Greenwoods Row car park in 1977. The array of buildings in the background has changed little.

Expo 84 – Grantham Trades Fair in May 1984 was held inside the former Ruston and Hornsby factory. This is Jim Baxter, who began with a junk shop at the former Hand and Hart pub, Wharf Road, which eventually became a bed shop.

Expo 84 – Grantham Trades Fair in May 1984. Sharpes Garden Shop was in Market Place, until it closed in 1986. The building later became a bar.

Tom Lambley's stand at the 1960 trades fair on the London Road sports ground, 'Grantham's own Olympia'. On display are the latest in domestic appliances.

Churches

Church of the Ascension

Lord Brownlow laid the foundation stone for the new church and church hall on Edinburgh Road, Harrowby, in July 1954. With him are, from left – architect Lawrence Bond, Mayor and Mayoress Coun and Mrs Ernest Hardy, Grantham vicar Canon Harold Leeke, Coun Gordon Foster and the Bishop of Grantham, the Rt Revd Tony Otter.

Volunteers level the ground before digging the foundations for the new Harrowby church in April 1954.

Worshippers leave Harrowby's new church in February 1956 following the dedication by the Bishop of Lincoln, the Rt Revd Kenneth Riches.

The Church of the Ascension, Harrowby, became the first Grantham church to open since St Anne's nearly 60 years earlier. The octagonal-shaped building was an extension to the dual purpose church/church hall built a year earlier. The £10,900 project was dedicated by the Bishop of Lincoln, the Rt Revd Kenneth Riches.

Church of the Epiphany

The Revd Jack Talent, priest-in-charge at Earlesfield, had to live in a 22ft x 7ft 6in caravan in 1955 because he had no vicarage. He also had to keep all his books there because there was no vestry in the church room, on the corner of The Grove and West Avenue. In the background workmen are building an extension to include a vestry.

The Revd Jack Talent was a familiar sight in the town with his black flowing cape. He would be seen mounted on a moped with a shopping basket on the front and frequently smoking a pipe. But things were looking up. In 1955 when these pictures were taken, work was already beginning on an extension to the Church of the Epiphany.

The old Humby bell found a new lease of life at the extension to the Church of the Epiphany in 1967. It was cast by Thomas Norris in 1639.

The new Church of the Epiphany, Earlesfield, under construction in June 1975.

Harrowby Lane Methodist

The story of a successful church is embodied in the short history of Harrowby Lane Methodist Church. It began as a wooden hut but in 1963 a bigger and permanent brick church was built in its place. By the end of the Millennium the congregation had outgrown even that one, so it was pulled down and another much larger one was built. It was opened in 2004.

Work continues on Harrowby Lane Methodist Church, as the new £10,000 brick building wraps itself around its timber predecessor in 1963.

Harrowby Lane Methodist Church was already obsolete in 1999.

The third church on the site, costing £760,000, was completed in 2004.

Finkin Street Methodist

A new organ costing £1,300 was installed in Finkin Street Methodist Church in 1951, to replace the one used since 1857. It had 1,414 pipes varying from 16ft to a mere inch long.

Secretary of State for Education and Science, Margaret Thatcher, was at a ceremony in Finkin Street Methodist Church in 1970 to dedicate a lectern in honour of her late father Alfred Roberts, who died earlier that year. Alderman Roberts had been a lay preacher as well as a councillor. Also there were his other daughter Muriel Cullen, his widow and ministers the Revd Bailey and the Revd Cox.

Finkin Street Methodist Church was literally under wraps for major roof and fabric repairs costing £40,000 in 1991. It was the first major overhaul for the building, erected in 1841, since the 1930s. The picture includes the Revd Joe Goodridge and steward Raymond Jackson.

The 100-strong Grantham Choral Society rehearses in Finkin Street Methodist Church for Handel's Messiah in 1997.

St Wulfram's Church

Vicar of Grantham Canon Harold Leeke (facing camera) in the vestry of St Wulfram's Church in 1954. With him are, from left, Sister Musson, the Revd E.C. Chandler (Harrowby), the Revd Jack Talent (Earlesfield) and the Revd Peter Rye. The vestry changed little over the centuries – apart from the addition of electricity.

An audience of 700 witnessed the first concert of Grantham Choral Society, which performed Handel's *Messiah* in St Wulfram's Church in 1963. This is the rehearsal. Although this was to celebrate the borough's quincentenary, they were still singing 50 years later.

Not so much a changing face as a different one. This model of St Wulfram's Church was made with 118,957 matchsticks by Ron Baker, of Oxford Street, in 1967. The model, which stood 55in high by 44in by 30in, took him seven years to build.

Choristers in St Wulfram's Church, with one of the building's fine stained-glass windows. Taken in 1985, it was the first colour picture to appear in the *Grantham Journal*.

St Anne's

Rome wasn't built in a day, and neither was St Anne's Church, Harrowby Road. It was officially opened in 1907 to replace the Tin Tabernacle but it wasn't completed until 1963. The back wall facing Hall's Hill was still corrugated iron, but this picture in December 1962 shows the brickwork nearing completion. The finishing touches cost £6,500.

St Anne's Church, Harrowby Road, held a pet service in October 1968 to celebrate the feast of St Francis of Assisi. Ironically, a former vicar of the church for some 40 years was the Revd Edwin Millard, known locally as Monkey Millard as he ran a small menagerie. The church was built in 1909, next door to the cemetery to replace a church further down the road known as the Tin Tabernacle. At the back of the picture is the vicar, the Revd A.G.B. Parsons, with his whippets and RSPCA inspector Tony Booth.

The Revd Timothy Kidd and Mayor Ron Briggs unveiled a model of St Anne's Church in 1963 to celebrate the building's final completion. The exhibition was in the nearby New Somerby Institute.

St Mary's Church

The Statue of Our Lady in St Mary's Church, North Parade, was crowned as part of the 1951 May Day celebration by May Queen Ann Murphy. Also there were parish priest Canon L.A. Arendzen and Fr P. Downey (kneeling).

The 1.75-tonne bell tower cupola being replaced on St Mary's bell tower, North Parade, in 1985. It brought restoration of the tower near completion.

Bridge End Road Wesleyan Chapel

A special sportsmen's service was held at the Wesleyan Chapel, Bridge End Road, in 1955. The building was originally funded by industrialist William Hornsby in 1875, but in 1966 it was demolished. In the pulpit is Boston United player-manager Ray Middleton, who spent 17 years as a Football League goalkeeper, many of them with Derby County, until injury shortened his career. With him are William 'Chucky' Durance, Grantham League chairman, and the Revd Allen Lees.

This interesting fresco was put outside Bridge End Road Wesleyan Chapel by the new chaplain, the Revd Allan J. Bowers (right), in 1957. It was inspired by one he had seen on a visit to the American Chapel Centre in Tokyo.

Other churches

Inside the Baptist Church, Wharf Road, in April 1960. Television company ATV were in Grantham for the weekend, to broadcast wrestling on Saturday and the Easter Sunday service next day.

Inside the Salvation Army Citadel, London Road, refurbished in 1981 at a cost of £7,800. It was just a century since the group came to Grantham. They had various meeting places, including the Theatre Royal, before building their own citadel in 1896.

The century-old organ in the United Reformed Church, Castlegate, was completely overhauled in 1986. The Revd Eric McDonald is watching workmen carry out the task.

The new Kingdom Hall, built by volunteers who converted a former malting on Brewery Hill. It had previously been a store for builders' merchants Jackson Shipley. The elders decided to move from the previous HQ on North Parade which became a play school.

Inside St John in Spittlegate Church as guides and brownies celebrated St George's Day in 1967.

Inside the new Kingdom Hall on Brewery Hill.

Sport & Leisure

Grantham Football Club

FORMED in 1874, Grantham FC has a colourful history. Having been in the Central Alliance and Midland League, the club competed in the Southern League in recent years, apart from a short spell in the Northern Premier. Their first FA Cup encounter was in 1877, losing to Clapham Rovers who went on to win the trophy three years later. The club shared the London Road ground with the town cricket club until the cricketers moved to Gorse Lane when landowners Buckminster Trust sold the site to Safeway for a supermarket. The football team played their last match on London Road in 1990 and after a year playing home matches at Spalding, settled at the South Kesteven Sports Stadium, Trent Road.

Player-manager Cyril Hatton and reserve-team skipper Doug Wallace were joined by ace marksman Jack Macartney and groundsman Bill Pearson to clear the lines at London Road before a match in March 1955. In the background are the poplars, a landmark on the ground for many years until they were felled after becoming diseased. Grantham were playing at Boston United. The reserves were at home to Brush Sports.

It was a tight squeeze going down towards the terraces at the London Road football ground. In August 1957, most men wore ties even for a football match but some, especially the younger men, began to dispense with headgear. About 2,400 fans turned out for this, the opening match of the season, Grantham v Worksop in the Midland League. A single Cyril Brown goal gave both points to Grantham.

A football match at the old London Road ground, renowned for its slope. In 1961, there was no concrete terracing at the top end, just ash. Along the left was the 'Shed', low-roofed and for standing only, as was the Witham (or Poplar) End at the far end. One of the ground's best known features was the row of poplar trees.

Concrete terracing replaced the pile of ashes which served Grantham FC fans at the 'top end' of the London Road football ground. It first came into use at Christmas 1966. The second-storey building was the press box.

Grantham Football Club players in the somewhat primitive dressing rooms at their London Road ground in 1967. These were a far cry from Old Trafford – or even the Meres stadium. These were former stables once belonging to the Blue Horse next door. In the centre is the physio's table. Players in the picture include Barrie Wood, John Small, George Jowett, Terry Bly, Tony Farmer, Hugh Wilson, Roy South, Cyril Brown and Ron Harrison.

Work began on the £3,000 covered terracing down the side of the London Road football ground in 1967 with the dismantling of the old 'scratching shed', a low structure with crude earth terracing and an odour all of its own. The timbers, despite their age, were found to be in excellent condition. In the background is Harrow Street, whose houses were also on borrowed time.

A new social club for football fans was nearly complete at the London Road football ground in January 1972. It was opened by popular Football League referee Roger Kirkpatrick. It became known as Grantham FC Sporting Club and for many years was the town's premier spot for both jazz and country and western music. In the foreground is the supporters' club tea kiosk.

Grantham FC on the London Road ground in 1982 with the 'new' stand in the background. From left are, back: Frank Baxter (director), John Toon, (director), Mike Harrold, Nigel Marshall (trainer), John Tandy, David Heal, Graham Cox, Brian Stubbs, Colin Foster, Tommy Young, Jock Turnbull (assistant trainer), David Boothman (chairman) and Howard Kilbourn (secretary). Front: Tim Thacker, Steve Hines, Jon Nixon (player-manager), Alan Jones, Dave Leadbeater and Bob Todd.

The cricket pavilion at London Road in 1985. It was opened by England and Yorkshire's Herbert Sutcliffe but destroyed by arsonists in 1990.

The new stand at the London Road football ground in 1985.

The new £4 million multi-sports stadium being built on the Meres, Trent Road, in 1991. The skeleton of the stand takes shape.

The Safeway supermarket nears completion on the site of the former London Road football and cricket ground in July 1991.

Dysart Park

Originally Houghton Road Recreation Ground, it was named after the Earl of Dysart who donated the land in 1926. It was turned into a formal park thanks to government grants as a way of giving the unemployed useful work. It included a bandstand, bowling greens, tennis courts, playground, playing field and an outdoor lido, which closed in 1980. The previous year, only 650 adults had used it following the opening of the town's indoor swimming pool.

A cedar tree was planted by Mayor Joseph Hardacre in Dysart Park in 1953. It was presented as a Coronation gift by children from Spitalgate School. Peering out of their windows and over the wall are residents of Houghton Road.

There was nothing like a nice warm day in Dysart Park swimming pool to cool down, as seen here in 1955. Unfortunately, spring time was not quite so warm.

Gordon Butters dives at the King's School 1957 swimming event held at Dysart Park Pool.

Dysart Park swimming pool in its heyday. The tower in the far corner was the entrance, through a turnstile, with an office above. The young ladies are the gala queen Mary Gailbraith and her assistants.

Dysart Park paddling pool on a balmy June day in 1970. Between the fence and the building at the rear ran the River Witham. The swimming pool was on the left.

Wyndham Park

Wyndham Park is the town's memorial to the fallen of the World War One. It was named after Captain Reginald Wyndham, whose winter home was on North Parade. He was the third son of Baron Leconfield and a lieutenant in the Life Guards, who was killed in action in Belgium in November 1914. The park was originally called Slate Mill Park, after the mill which stood where White Bridge is now. Wyndham Park was less formal than Dysart Park. The swimming pool pre-dated the park and was formed by diverting the river. It closed in 1971 and seven years later became a skateboard park. As the craze diminished, it was refilled with water and became home to Grantham Model Boat Club. When skateboarding made a revival, a new area was developed on the eastern end of the top playing field.

Wyndham Park paddling pool has always been popular with youngsters and little seems to have changed since 1957 apart from the style of the costumes.

Wyndham Park in 1935 when children spelled out the town's name to celebrate 100 years of a town council. A certain Margaret Hilda Roberts, of Huntingtower Road School, is in the 'M'. Outside the park, housing development seems a long way off. Regrettably much of the open land has since been filled in.

They bred them tough in 1952 when indoor swimming pools were unheard of. Instead, even in May, hundreds would turn out at Wyndham Park to enjoy the great outdoors. The grassy bank on the riverside was always an attraction. The ground around sometimes got muddy and slippery, most people at sometime stubbed their toes on the concrete surround and the steps were slippery painted wood.

A chilly 52 degrees Fahrenheit (11 degrees Celsius) failed to stop enthusiastic swimmers on the first day of the season in May 1962. These lads helped to set a first day attendance record at the Wyndham Park pool.

Wyndham Park swimming pool, also in May 1952, showing the footbridge at the end. This became very slippery with the mix of leaves from the trees and many wet feet.

Scouts and Cubs paraded in Wyndham Park in 1953, about 500 of them together with Guides and Brownies. Their chaplain, the Revd E.E. Jourdain, led the prayers. In the background is the nursery school, opened in wartime to help women work in industry. It was replaced by a brick building at the end of the 20th century.

Wyndham Park swimming pool closed following the introduction of the indoor pool. In 1978 it was converted into a skateboard park.

Vandals are nothing new, as this bench in 1970 Wyndham Park shows. But play was far more dangerous, with concrete flagstones the only thing to break the fall of these children.

Thirty trees affected by Dutch elm disease, which was sweeping the country in 1979, had to be felled in Wyndham Park.

This road roller was presented to the town in the early 1960s by Eddison Plant for children to play on. It was found a place in Wyndham Park and thrilled generations. Unfortunately, due to an accident to a child, South Kesteven District Council was forced to withdraw it in 1999. In the background is Little Gonerby School and Hill Avenue beyond.

Inside the quincentenary swimming pool which opened in November 1971.

Quincentenary Memorial Pool/Union Street Leisure Centre

The decision to create an indoor swimming pool in 1963 to celebrate the 500th anniversary of the town's charter took nine years to come to fruition. It was finally built in Union Street after various sites, including Wyndham Park and the Paddock off Stonebridge Road, were considered. Unfortunately, the design of an upstairs pool was not 100 percent successful. Ten years later, footballer Trevor Brooking opened the £1 million leisure centre which was incorporated into the building. In the 1990s, a £9 million complex was built on Trent Road and Union Street was sold to Asda, who built a superstore on the site.

The first water was pumped into the Union Street indoor swimming pool for testing purposes in 1971.

There was a bleak outlook for anyone sitting outside Grantham Leisure Centre, Union Street, in 1982. Anyone fed up with sitting looking at four walls at home could sit outside and look at just one. A spokesman for South Kesteven District Council, which installed the seats, saw nothing wrong. He said: 'We faced the seats that way to avoid people looking at the dilapidated buildings opposite.'

The quincentenary swimming pool ready to open in November 1971.

Meres Leisure Centre

Opened in 1998, the Meres Leisure Centre was without doubt the best in the county, if not the East Midlands. The Trent Road site already had a football and athletics stadium, indoor bowling club and table tennis centre, so the £9 million building was the icing on the cake for a super sports complex.

The Meres Leisure Centre had taken on a very futuristic look by August 1997.

The pool area inside the new leisure centre in October 1997.

The leisure lagoon at the leisure centre in 1998.

Grantham Indoor Bowling Club was built on the Meres in 1982, mainly through donations from members.

The Meres Leisure Centre ready for the opening in 1998.

Cinema

The Compton organ at the Granada cinema was legendary. For many films it appeared from below stage with its full lighting. It was a great favourite on Saturday mornings, too, for the Granadiers children's cinema club. It was played here by Mike Hall, of the Boys' Central School, to celebrate his 13th birthday in 1967. Mike went on to become a professional organist.

Last days of the Granada in 1988. A hole had been knocked in the side wall off Bath Street for demolition contractors to get their equipment in.

Half of the Granada was rubble by March 1988. All that remains is the balcony, the front seats of which were reserved on Saturday mornings for Granadiers – junior cinema club members – whose birthdays were that week.

Screen 2 opened at the Paragon, St Catherine's Road, in 1988, featuring the Last Emperor. Seated is owner Robin Sanders.

Workmen put the finishing to the interior of the Paragon Cinema in March 1983.

The Picture House gave way to progress, becoming a Tesco supermarket in 1961. The nearby Rainbow milk and snack bar, once very popular with teenagers, became an electrical store soon after.

Education

Grantham College

Minister of Education Florence Horsbrugh laid the foundation stone for the Grantham College extension in November 1952. With her are, from left: Sir Robert Pattinson, Lt Cmdr J. Cracroft-Amcotts, county education chief Dr T.W.P. Golby and Bishop of Grantham the Rt Revd Anthony Otter.

G.F. Johnson, principal of Grantham College, inspecting a model of the new college in 1954 with county architect J.W.H. Barnes. The budget for the project was £77,000.

Students learn typing at Grantham College in 1981, using what was then the latest technology.

The official opening of the final instalment of Grantham College of Further Education in 1959. From left: principal George F. Johnson, naturalist Peter Scott who formally opened it and director of education Dr T.W.P. Golby.

King's School

The Bishop of London, Dr J.W.C. Wand, unveiled a memorial in 1951 in the Old School, Grantham King's School, in memory of old boys killed in World War Two. An old boy himself, he was there for the school's Founders Day service.

The timber building which had served as classrooms, including the art department, at the King's School, Brook Street, since 1918, was finally demolished in 1968. It made way for a new three-storey extension costing £100,000.

Chairman of governors Alderman J. Hedley-Lewis drove in the ceremonial peg for the King's School's £21,000 swimming pool in February 1969. The house (left) is the rear of St Wulfram's Rectory.

King's School indoor swimming pool, measuring 20m by 30m, opened in July 1969. It was filled but it was so near the end of term it was September before it came into use.

Kesteven and Grantham Girls' School

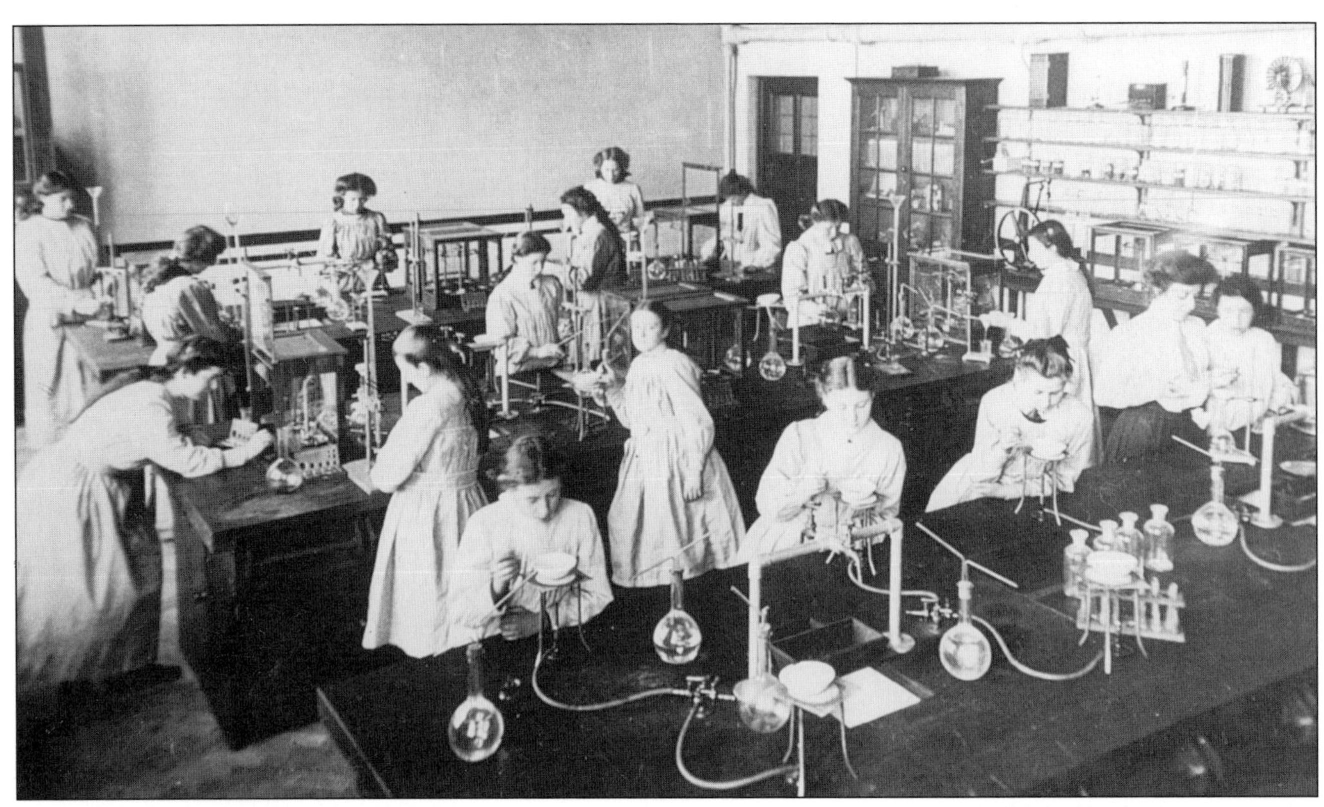

Girls in the laboratory at the newly opened Kesteven and Grantham Girls' School in 1910. Little did they know that one pupil would later distinguish herself in chemistry before going on to become Prime Minister.

Kesteven and Grantham Girls' School celebrate the school's Golden Jubilee in October 1960.

Kesteven and Grantham Girls' School used their brand new hall for the first time in February 1986. The hall completed a number of additions at the school including a new block with seven laboratories, four practical rooms and a classroom. The main school was also upgraded. The picture shows headteacher Miss Wilson addressing the pupils. It was opened later in the year by Prime Minister and old girl Margaret Thatcher.

St Hugh's High School

Earlesfield Secondary Modern School (later St Hugh's), costing £180,000, nears completion in February 1960.

Earlesfield in miniature made by students at St Hugh's School, with their school as the centrepiece.

Boys' Central School

The Revd E.E. Jourdain at the Boys' Central School, Hill Avenue, dedicating the lectern and refectory table made in the school's woodwork room in 1951. George Neal and Colin Stephens were the carpenters, working under the direction of woodwork master Mr V.E. 'Ben' Sewell and Mr E. Bowden.

Sir John Hunt, who led the successful expedition to conquer Mount Everest in 1953. He visited the Boys' Central School (later Little Gonerby School), Hill Avenue, to present boys with their Duke of Edinburgh awards in 1961. He's walking up the 'quad', as it was known.

The Boys' Central School left Hill Avenue in 1978 after 58 years. In the background is the HORSA block, a temporary concrete building, introduced in 1948 when the school leaving age was raised to 15. HORSA stood for Hutting Operation for the Raising of School-leaving Age. The premises were taken over by Little Gonerby Infants' School.

The new Boys' Central School opened on Rushcliffe Road in April 1978. It was still all boys (380 boys and 20 staff). Girls were introduced in September.

Grantham Church School

St Wulfram's School (later Grantham Church School) under construction in 1954. It was planned to hold 650 children and was more than 100 yards long. The modern design would say goodbye to bricklaying. The same plans were used at Billingborough, Billinghay and Corby Glen, although the schools were built at different angles making them appear more individual.

Work began on the indoor swimming pool at St Wulfram's School, Queensway, in May 1970.

Susan Speechley and Joan Chambers were the first to take the plunge in St Wulfram's School pool in December 1970. It cost £4,186 19s 3d to build.

Blessed Hugh More School

Blessed Hugh More School, Tennyson Avenue, was set for closure in 1987.

Blessed Hugh More School closed in July 1989. Headteacher Mary Lewis said: 'Kenneth Baker didn't see us as a viable school.' There were 78 pupils.

In 1993 the decision was made to pull down the former Blessed Hugh More School buildings as they were a target for vandals.

Springfield County Secondary School

Springfield County Secondary School opened its new hall and gymnasium in July 1961, a bargain at £20,000. Inside, it was fully equipped with changing rooms and showers. With comfortable seating it could hold 350 people. It became incorporated into Huntingtower Primary School.

Tony Clark is watched by girls wearing pinnies as he ices a cake in domestic science at Springfield County Secondary School, Huntingtower Road, in 1955. The concrete classrooms were very utilitarian, with metal windows, overhead water pipes and primitive electrics. Huntingtower Primary School eventually expanded on to the site.

Other Schools

The National School took the plunge by installing a gas-heated swimming pool, 33ft by 25ft, in 1969. It cost £2,000.

Spitalgate School began in Launder Terrace in 1844 and after a spell at Stonebridge House, St Catherine's Road, moved to new premises in Trent Road in 1977. Here, the new building nears completion.

Little Gonerby Infants' School closed after 120 years. Built in 1863 on the junction of New Street and Albion Street, it was originally a school chapel costing the Revd Richard Cust £800. It became a school two years later, the children moving from Union Street, and a second storey was added. After the pupils departed for the former Boys' Central School in 1985 it became a residential home.

Little Gonerby Infants' School in 1985, which took over the former Boys' Central School, Sandon Road. There were many changes including the demolition of the HORSA block, building in the corridors and putting the toilets inside.

Walton Girls' High School opened on Kitty Briggs Lane in 1966, replacing the Girls' Central School, which occupied a building in Castlegate and the former Brownlow School, Finkin Street, for 45 years. Headmistress Nina Hewitt, in charge since 1946, was still only the school's second headmistress, having taken over from Miss Jabet.

In 1968 the roof of Gonerby Hill Foot School crashed to the floor an hour before 100 pupils were expected to be at their desks. Caretaker Ellen Latter saw water leaking through and put buckets down to catch the water, but when she returned the ceiling collapsed just as she opened the door. Headteacher Miss D. Moulding allowed the children the rest of the day off.

A rare photograph of Welby Street Infants' School. Until the demolition of the John Lee factory in 1983, it was hardly in view. A month later, nothing was left but rubble and a foundation stone built into the Isaac Newton Centre.

Children at Harrowby Infants' School proved they had road sense as they carried out a traffic routine in the school playground at an open day in July 1962. Headteacher Miss M.E. Pick was very keen on road safety.

Pupils at St Anne's School were short of space as they moved out of their Victorian stone building on Dudley Road for a new one on Harrowby Road. The building wasn't ready by September 1973, so some of the children had to learn in the church.

The temporary school toilets at St Anne's Church were not what they should have been.

Wyndham Park Day Nursery had occupied a timber building since it opened during World War Two. It was meant to allow mothers to concentrate on war work. This picture was taken in 1997 when the brand new £350,000 centre opened.

Transport

Grantham Bypass

THE A1 Grantham bypass was begun in 1960 and took two years to complete. The £2 million road was opened in early August 1962 to cope with the August Bank Holiday traffic. August Bank Holiday Monday was the first Monday of the month in those days.

The Grantham bypass, as seen from Gorse Lane in 1960. By April there was an earth road running the six-mile length as 200 workmen laboured around the clock.

Grantham bypass seen from the air in September 1960. The slip road on to Harlaxton Road is marked out in earth and the flyover parapets are in place. Under the wing tip is the Grantham Canal, which borders fields now covered by Earlesfield estate and industrial estates.

Two 60ft mobile cranes, each worth £15,000, raised 16 26-tonne concrete beams into place to form the parapets for the Harlaxton Road flyover.

Grantham to Nottingham traffic was carried over the A1 Grantham bypass for the first time in July 1961, when the A52 flyover was complete.

Looking southwards from the Barrowby Road flyover in August 1962. Not only is there little traffic, there is little sign of roadside development. It was built using a revolutionary concrete laying system, developed by Lord Hailsham's Department of Scientific and Industrial Research road laboratory. This picture was taken the day before the road opened to traffic.

In 2001, the bridge carrying Dysart Road over the A1 was knocked down and rebuilt. This is the temporary footbridge while work was carried out.

Future Prime Minister Sir Anthony Eden buying some reading matter from WH Smith's bookstall at Grantham railway station in 1951.

Railway

Engine driver Matthew Hudson (centre) retired from the railway in 1954 after 50 years, 25 of them as a main line driver. He drove both King George VI and Winston Churchill. He was driver of the *Aberdonian* in 1946 when it derailed at 60mph at Hatfield, running upright 120 yards along the sleepers. Being a top link driver was highly regarded in the days of steam.

Members of Grantham Townswomen's Guild met outside Grantham Railway Station. They were off to London for a visit to the House of Commons and the Ideal Home Exhibition at Olympia in 1955. The picture is interesting for a study in fashion. No trainers or tracksuit bottoms for these ladies on a trip to the capital city. All are wearing hats, most wear gloves and some are even wearing fur coats.

A train with 27 wagons carrying a £132,000 export order for Aveling Barford destined for Buenos Aires, Argentina, in the sidings at Grantham. It was then the biggest order placed by the South American country outside the USA. The picture also shows how busy the railways were in those days, as well as the landmark coal tower.

Another Aveling Barford special train, this time loaded with 32 dyke cleaners, destined for Poland, in 1960. The building on the right is the old granary. Most of these sidings were ripped up to make way for car parking in the 1990s.

A 120-ton steam locomotive ended its days when in 1963 it was shunted into the sidings of Grantham scrap merchants F.C. Larkinson for breaking. The 21-year-old locomotive, number 63982, built in 1942, took 10 days to dismantle. The wheels alone weighed four tons, and the steel was sent for remelting in Birmingham furnaces.

Hundreds of people lined the platform of Grantham station to see the *Flying Scotsman* in March 1983.

The East Coast Main Line took on a wintry mantle in January 1982. The picture was taken from South Parade bridge.

Grantham railway station in 1985.

Inside the modernised booking office at Grantham railway station in 1985.

The pedestrian tunnel beneath the railway, an old right of way from the town centre and always gloomy.

Outside Grantham railway station in 1985.

Bus Station

When it was time for a bus to leave, the driver and conductor would magically appear from the tiny staff canteen at the bus station. Sometimes it was like Dr Who's Tardis, the way so many came out of there. The picture was taken in 1953.

There is so much going on in this picture, it seems strange it was inspired by people stopping work. The schoolboys in their caps (you could be caned for failing to wear one), a lad going fishing, a proud ex-serviceman with his badge and blazer. Behind is the waiting room, which was locked out of hours. They had a long wait, as this was during a lightning strike in 1953.

Even in austere times, ladies dressed up to go to town, although they were displeased when they discovered there was no way home. They were stranded by a drivers' strike in 1953.

GENTS

OMNIBUS
STATION
10

A school bus is allowed to leave the strike-torn bus station in 1953, but shoppers were left stranded. Behind Platform 10 is the old police station, before it moved to Stonebridge, St Catherine's Road.

Members of Nottingham Forest Supporters' Club gathered at Grantham bus station heading for Munich for their team's European Cup final against Swedish club Malmo in 1979. The trip cost them £40 a head.

Wharf Road Bus Station in 1998.

The toilet block and shop at the old bus station, St Peter's Hill, are pulled down to make way for the £1.5 million district council building.

Other Transport

The Co-op coal lorry had a small altercation with a vehicle from Peterborough in 1955. The police patrolman watches as they attempt to untangle the mess. Coalmen were tough cookies. They had to carry those hundredweight (50kg) sacks from their lorries to the customers' coal houses which were often down a long passage and at the end of a yard.

Motorcycle patrolmen were inspected by the Inspector of Constabularies at Stonebridge, the Grantham Division HQ, in July 1962. He was accompanied by Chief Constable J. Barnett, Assistant Chief Constable A. Johnson and Grantham Division Superintendent T.F. Travis.

Grantham Motor Company, one of the town's oldest motor dealers, secured an order for 10 Ford Escorts for Lincolnshire Police in 1968. The new Panda cars, worth £15,000, were for use by beat bobbies as opposed to the traffic department, which was equipped with higher powered vehicles. Grantham Motors moved from London Road to new premises on Spittlegate Level in the 1980s. It was demolished in the late 1990s to become a small retail park.

Public buildings

Guildhall

The Sessions Hall in 1985 before it became the Guildhall Arts Centre theatre. The room was then used by Grantham magistrates, the county court and the charter trustees as well as being the dojo for the judo club.

The Guildhall in 2003, with the small hedge still in place on St Peter's Hill green. The building was erected in 1868 and remains largely unchanged outside.

The Queen Mother on an official visit to Grantham in 1963 to celebrate the town's quincentenary, in the Sessions Hall. Next to her is the Mayor, Ron Briggs.

A new cap is lowered on top of the Guildhall with the help of a 130ft crane in 1972. The new copper cap replaced the former wrought-iron one. At the back is well-known local cricket umpire Vic Heppenstall.

Police cells at the Guildhall, built in 1868 as an overnight lock-up. The building, pictured here in 1986, was incorporated into the box office of the Guildhall Arts Centre.

Civic Centre

It may seem odd now, but when this first phase of the new civic centre on St Peter's Hill was completed in 1967, the next move planned was to demolish the Guildhall. The library and museum were also to be bulldozed and the facilities incorporated into the new complex. Inside the railings was Abbey Gardens.

Contractors complete last-minute checks to the electronic voting system in the new council chamber, St Peter's Hill, in 1987.

Post Office

Betty Widdowson with postmaster A.G. Stewart and Mayor Lloyd Ramsden. She is buying one of the first Premium Bonds at Grantham Post Office in October 1956. Three positions were dedicated to the new bonds to cope with the anticipated sales. But the old post office was an unfriendly place, as grilles had yet to be replaced by the more friendly reinforced glass.

Grantham Telephone exchange at the Post Office in 1953. The 24 girls worked 8am to 6pm with 17 men taking over the night shift. Together they handled 5,000 calls a day, 2,000 of them local. At peak times they handled 500 calls an hour.

Inside the sleek new post office in November 1969.

Apart from the strange sight of elephants parading towards St Catherine's Road, this is an excellent view of the former general post office. This oversized 'charm bracelet' was from Sir Robert Fossett's Circus, performing in Wyndham Park in 1957.

The Mayor and Mayoress, Councillor and Mrs Herbert Harris, and their son John, visit Grantham sorting office at their peak period just before Christmas in 1964.

The new general post office opened on St Peter's Hill in 1969, using the standard 'house style'. The unique feature was the retention of the holly trees. The GPO planned to install outdoor seating in the area. The post office had been in the Market Place until 1922, when it moved to St Peter's Hill. The building on the corner of Wharf Road had yet to be demolished to make way for the new sorting office van park.

Pickets outside the sorting office, Wharf Road, during a strike in 1988.

Postman Kevin Hardy, 19, in his smart uniform, received a packet delivery trolley that made back-breaking deliveries by a sack over the shoulder a thing of the past.

Library

Youngsters were queuing up to take out books at Grantham children's library in 1954. The children's library was separated by a glass partition from the adults' section. More than 1,000 books a year were being read by youngsters. Librarian Percy Willard said: 'The gap between a horror comic and even the lightest story is quite enormous. You cannot beat a healthy read.'

Inside Grantham's new library, built to accommodate 45,000 volumes. It cost £238,000 when it opened in 1984, above the Isaac Newton shopping centre.

Grantham Hospital

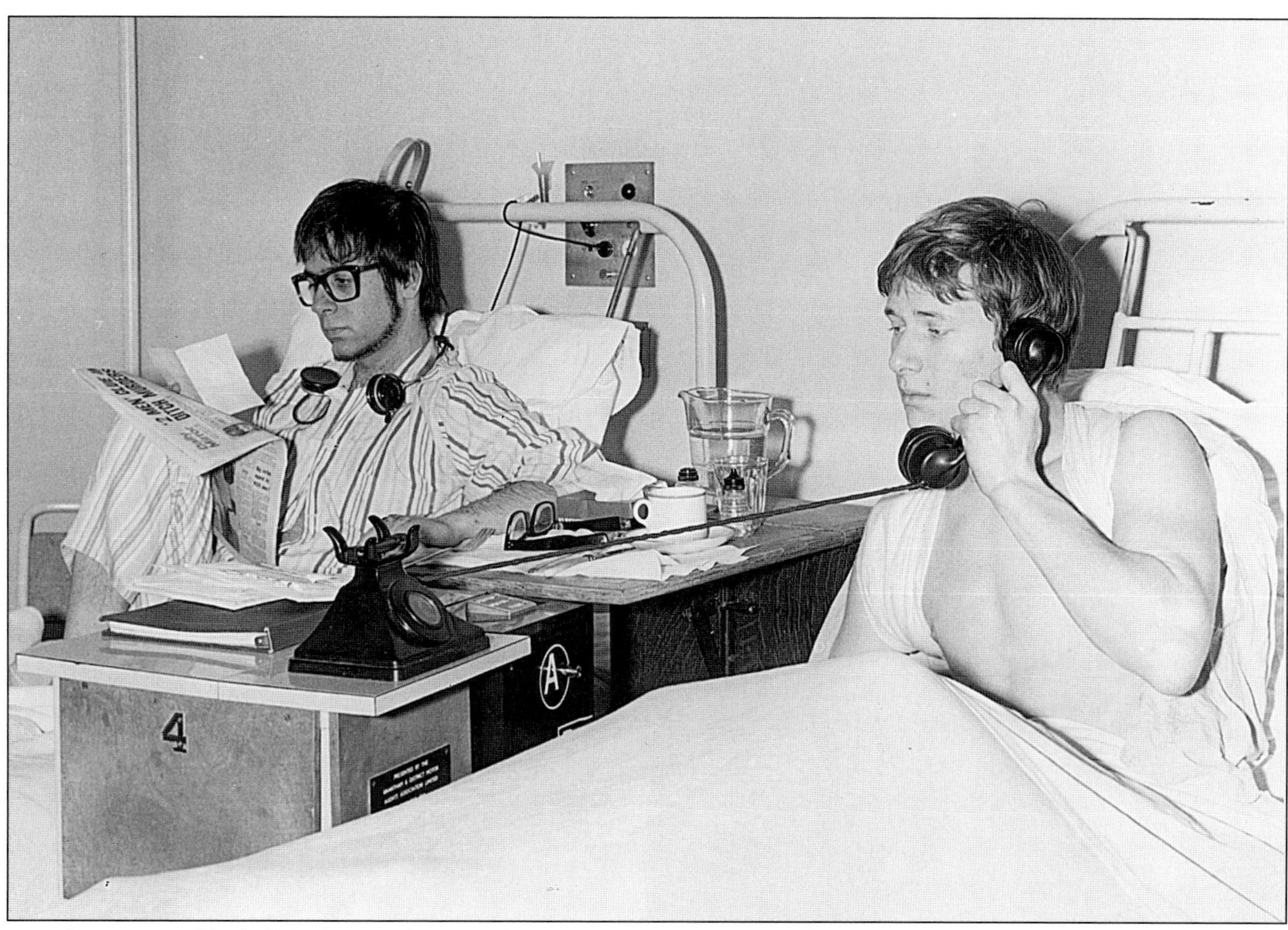

Grantham Hospital had all the latest technology for the comfort of patients, including a mobile payphone. Then, of course, there was hospital radio, with the not-so-miniature headsets. And should the patients look familiar, that's because it's Manfred Mann and his singer Paul Jones in January 1966 when they were recovering from a road accident just outside town.

If you are trying to guess where the photographs were taken before looking at the captions, this one probably foxed you. They are the newly-built nurses' flats at Grantham Hospital on the east side of Manthorpe Road, in 1970. Two blocks each had accommodation for 20 student nurses; a third had room for 27 staff and state-enrolled nurses and the fourth for 15 various staff. They were pulled down 30 years later for a housing development.

The state-of-the-art maternity/gynaecology department costing £440,000 opened at Grantham Hospital in July 1972. It was designed for 48 maternity patients and was one of the tallest buildings in Grantham.

Grantham Hospital showing the wooden huts making up the departments in 1976. It took a pounding from the Lincolnshire Community Health Council, the health service watchdog. Although staff, food and cleanliness were praised, the operating was found wanting with no recovery room. There was an eight-month wait for X-rays and then there were those departments still housed in temporary wooden huts.

Grantham Hospital seen from the maternity wing.

An RAF helicopter ready to take a road accident victim to Stoke Mandeville Hospital, exposing a rare view of Grantham Hospital in 1986.

The original Grantham Hospital, built in 1876, photographed in 1991.

The new extensions at Grantham and District General Hospital in 1959. The spacious, well-equipped wards accommodating up to 80 patients cost £300,000.

Cattle Market

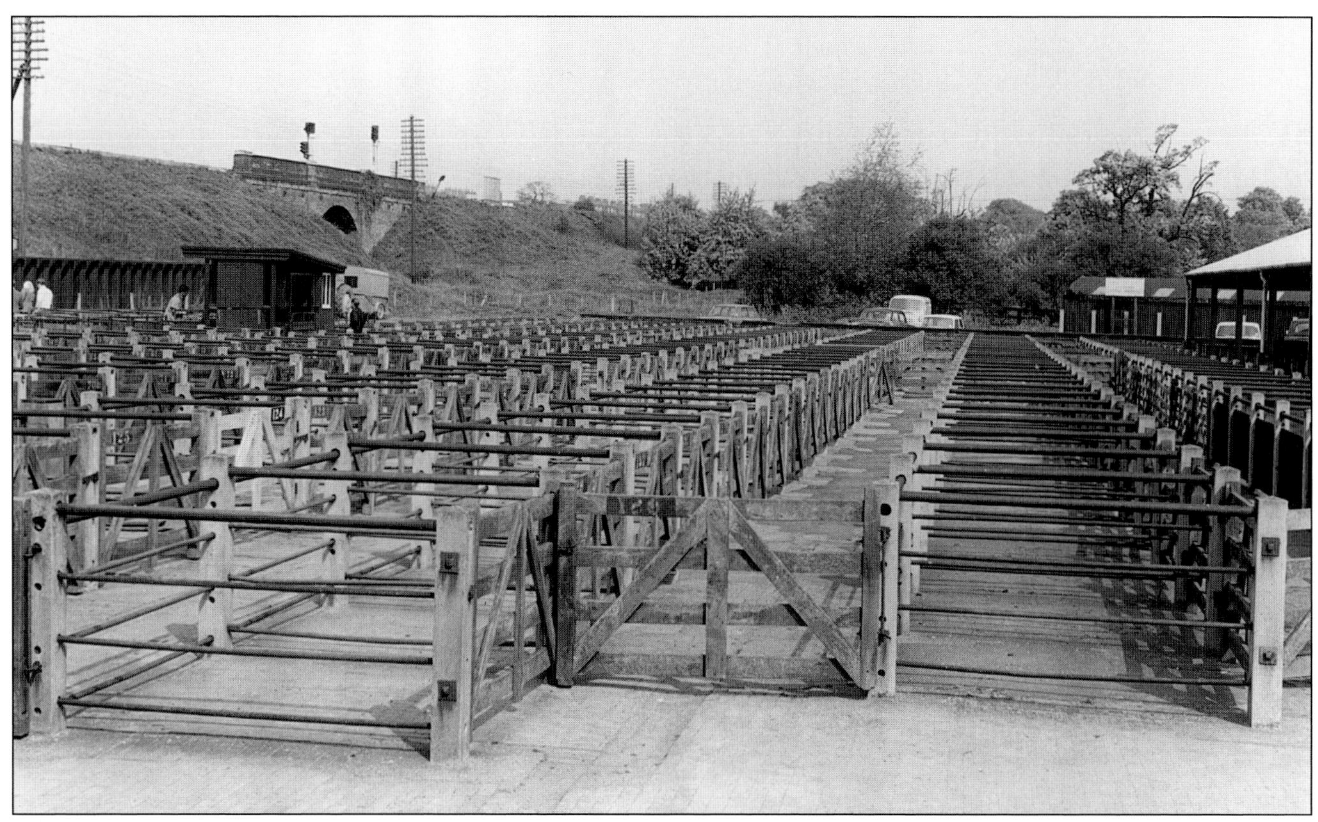

Grantham Cattle Market in 1970. Much of this area became Sankt Augustin Way.

Farmers and butchers at Grantham Cattle Market auction in 1992, where a bull decides to make a bid for freedom.

Other Buildings

Chandos House, Gorse Rise, was opened by the Queen Mother in 1963. This is in December 1962 as the £48,400 old people's complex was nearing completion. It had accommodation for 42 residents.

Harrison House on Dysart Road was opened in 1970 by Alderman J.W. Harrison after whom it was named. It provided accommodation for 40 senior citizens. The complex cost £83,749 to build and a further £8,000 to furnish.

Welby Everard Court, at the bottom of College Street, opened in March 1975. There were 20 single flats and two doubles. The clergyman is Rector of Grantham, Canon Graham Sansbury. Rent at the new Royal British Legion flats was set at £8.35 for a single occupant and £11.31 for a couple. The complex cost £95,000.

The new community centre at Canterbury Close, Queensway, in 1976.

Grantham House, Castlegate, once known as Hall Place, is one of Grantham's oldest habitable buildings. With his labradors is the tenant in 1996, Major General Sir Brian Wyldbore-Smith.

Beaconfield clinic, Beacon Lane, taken in 1994. Originally a private house, for many years it was a children's clinic treating everything from flat feet to protruding teeth. In the late 20th century it became part of a mental health unit.

Emergency Services

Police

Grantham police officers demonstrate the new lightweight personal radios which were to revolutionise policing in 1966.

Police introduced new uniforms in 1969. PC Harry Kime (left) is wearing the previous one and the new look is modelled by PC Gareth Williams.

Fire

Members of Kesteven Fire Service tried out a new fire hose, so pliable it made work easy. Each of the 16ft sections made of polythene weighed a mere 50lb and would replace the cast-iron pipes that were in service. On a hot day in September 1954, firemen in their double-breasted tunics laid 55 lengths – 880ft – around Buckminster Gardens to show how easy it was.

Waterways

Grantham Canal

Two generations enjoy skating on the frozen Grantham Canal towards Swing Bridge in February 1956. In those days, the harder winters meant it was worthwhile buying skates and toboggans. In the background is Harlaxton Road and beyond is the site of Walton Girls' High School and the Denton Avenue development, about to be started.

Schoolboys enjoy an afternoon in February 1956 on the Grantham Canal. Behind them is the area known as 'The Willows', which were grown as osier beds by W.B. Harrison in Victorian times.

Members of Grantham Civic Trust and youngsters with the rubbish taken out of the Grantham Canal near Earlesfield Lane bridge in 1969.

Earlesfield youngsters cleaning up the Grantham Canal near Earlesfield Lane bridge in 1969.

Grantham Canal was again in the limelight as fish were dying due to the lack of oxygen in August 1974. The works on the left, probably part of the gasworks, have since been pulled down.

British Waterways workmen moved to the Grantham Canal with dredging equipment for a massive clean-up around Earlesfield Lane bridge in August 1980. They spent two weeks removing rubbish and debris from the section.

River Witham

Riverside Walk from the footbridge in Witham Place in January 1956. A 20ft wide riverside walk was promised by the borough council although it was expected to take 30 years to come to fruition. The walk was from Witham Place to Harrow Street and would eventually be extended to St Catherine's Road. By the late 1990s it had reached Harrowby Mill.

A van plunged into the River Witham from Bridge End Road bridge in December 1962 after running out of control down Somerby Hill. No one was hurt. To the left are the backs of houses in Witham Place, demolished to make way for an elderly people's complex which carried on the name. The maltings on the right is in Bridge Street.

River Witham widening to alleviate flooding in 1975. This stretch is behind Belton Lane.

The White Bridge, Wyndham Park, is partially demolished for river widening in 1975. The left span is shorter than the right as this was originally the site of Slate Mill, a water mill destroyed by fire in the 1890s.

River Witham widening near the island in Wyndham Park.

Pubs and Hotels

Public Houses

Florence Sophie Ogden celebrated her 88th birthday with friends in the Royal Oak, Market Place in 1957. Mrs Ogden, who lived in Union Street, had been a regular at the Market Place pub for 35 years. Serving the ladies in the snug is landlady Ivy Lake (standing).

The White Hart, High Street, before major refurbishment by owners Holes Brewery, of Newark, in 1957.

Days for the White Hart Hotel, High Street, were numbered in April 1986. The popular hostelry was soon to be replaced by a building society and a McDonald's restaurant.

The unusually named pub The Fletchers, Westgate, in 1986. Originally, and for about 150 years, it was called Frederick Fletcher and at one time had a no-Sunday licence which forced it to close at 9pm midweek. It was also nicknamed the Fur and Feathers and had a snug nicknamed the Gin Palace (and worse). Eventually it changed its name to the Market Cross and more recently the Establishment.

Inside the Gatehouse which opened in the former ironmongers Collards in 1987. The building was erected in about 1760. It later became The Playhouse.

The King's Arms reverted to the name when it first opened in the early 1700s. The Westgate pub had for more than a century been the Blue Ram, one of 14 'Blue' pubs in town. Among the alterations at the relaunch of the King's Arms in 1991 was reopening the archway, which had been filled in to make an extra room.

The 400-year-old Black Dog, Watergate, had a £550,000 facelift by owners Mansfield Brewery in 1997.

The Rose Castle pub, Trent Road, as seen by a bungee jumper in 1997.

The Tom Cobleigh pub, Barrowby Road, under construction. Eventually it became the Muddle Go Nowhere.

The Sportsman, Dysart Road. Built in 1968 as Coles Cranes Social Club, it later became a pub but was demolished in 2000 for housing.

Stella, Dawn and Helen Benton, who won a *Journal* competition in 1986. Behind them the White Hart Hotel is being demolished to make way for a McDonald's restaurant and the Melton Mowbray Building Society.

The Red Lion Hotel, High Street, was one of the town's most popular watering holes and drinkers were in mourning when it was demolished in 1963. But the hotel did not go down without a fight and firefighters were called to a mystery blaze as it was being pulled down. The fire engine is also worth more than a glance.

Odds & Sods

Parker's Field, Bath Field or Sedgwick Meadows

A snowy Bath Fields in 1955 with Agnes Street in the background to the right. The street was demolished in the 1960s, making way for the Riverside grouped old people's homes. On the left is Grantham College.

It was great fun when the snow fell every winter. These lads were sledging in Bath Fields, also known as Parker's Field, and later Sedgwick Meadows in 1955.

Sundry

Grantham Pimpernels Carnival Band was formed in 1952 and performed at all kinds of events from village fetes to major parades in the town, dressed in scarlet uniforms trimmed with white. They also played at Cleethorpes, Mablethorpe and Skegness. They disbanded in 1964. This picture was taken in June 1956, outside the Westgate Hall.

Distinguished-looking Grantham town councillors and aldermen (wearing gowns) in 1935 with the Mayor, Lord Brownlow in the centre (front). They are, from left, back: F.P. Digby, G.W. Green, Alf Barnett, R.R. Dale, and H. Quilter. Third row: J.W. Smith, Lilian Basford, Herbert Hopkin, B.H. Sindall, D. Sharpley, Mrs S.A. Barnes and William Goodliff. Second row: Stanley Foster, E.K. Trotter, A. Holmes, M.E. Osborn, Arthur Eatch and Alfred Roberts. Front row: Rothwell Lee, H. Beeden, Theo Rowle, Fred Weekly, R. Brittain, and W.E. Sharpe.

Frank Melton was appointed Grantham's first traffic warden in 1966. There was no excuse for parking in St Catherine's Road with a free car park across the road.

Housing Estates

Earlesfield

These were the first of 103 houses to be built on the Earlesfield estate by W.J. Roberts, of Bottesford. They were handed over to Councillor Tom Smith (dark suit), the borough council's chairman of housing, in July 1961. They were finished at the rate of 14 per month. The rent was £2 13s 0d (£2.65) including rates.

Aire Road flats in 1985. Built in 1961, they were in line for a £75,000 refurbishment. Nineteen years later they were scheduled for demolition.

This one takes some thinking about and it is difficult to find your bearings. In the foreground, to the left, are Aire Road flats. In 1962, when this was taken, there was plenty of land available for development at Earlesfield.

Teenagers at Earlesfield got fed up of waiting for the council to build them a youth centre at Hill View Adventure Playground, so in 1976 they created their own. Using old pallets, corrugated sheeting, felt and carpets they managed to make a waterproof structure which they furnished with old chairs and sofas people had thrown out.

Earlesfield gardens were open plan until the district council decided in 1977 to spend £33,000 to provide fences for the tenants. This picture was taken just before work began and the little dog was free to roam wherever he pleased.

Beeden Park

Trent Road came to a halt in 1981 – still divided from Harlaxton Road by the Grantham Canal. But plans were in hand to build a bridge to make it easier to get to Springfield Road.

A showhouse at Beechcroft Road following a £309,000 programme of improvements on Beeden Park in 1988, which included putting pitched roofs on the former flat-tops.

Harrowby

D.S. Connor's shop stood on Harrowby Lane for many years, close to the Methodist church. This picture was taken in the 1950s when it was busy. It is now a private house.

A rather frugal celebration by today's standards for the Queen's Coronation in June 1953, with plenty of egg and cress sandwiches, jam tarts, and orange juice. This street party was in the newly-built Shakespeare Avenue.

Eight shops with flats over were completed to serve 4,000 tenants in the Harrowby area. The complex was built by Foster & Son for £21,779 8s 2d. First tenants were the Co-op, Mrs Porter (hairdresser), G.A. Emitt (butcher), J.H. Baker (greengrocer), J.E. Jessop (barber), Forbuoys (newsagent) and L.K. Coaten (fish and chips). In the background is Harrowby Infants' School, now obscured from this angle by a block of flats.

St Wulfram's verger Arthur Nidd leads the way along Harrowby Lane to the laying of the foundation stone for the Church of the Ascension, Edinburgh Road, in 1954. Behind him is cross-bearer Ron Weightman with St Wulfram's Guild of Servers.

A coal cart parked at Pensions Corner, New Beacon Road, ended up a wreck in Harrowby Lane in August 1958. The horse was frightened and bolted, losing the cart shortly afterwards on Harrowby Lane, just past the Princess Drive junction. It was chased by RSPCA officer Inspector C. Marshall in his van along Harrowby Road, Bridge End Road, and was finally caught on Houghton Road.

A lorry belonging to coal merchants Parson Bros and Snape ran away and crashed into the side of a Queensway bungalow. It began its journey at the top of Melbourne Road. That was in 1963.

A round-the-houses cycle race organised by Witham Wheelers in 1963 to celebrate the town's quincentenary. The pack is riding up Princess Drive, followed by a brand new Morris Minor.

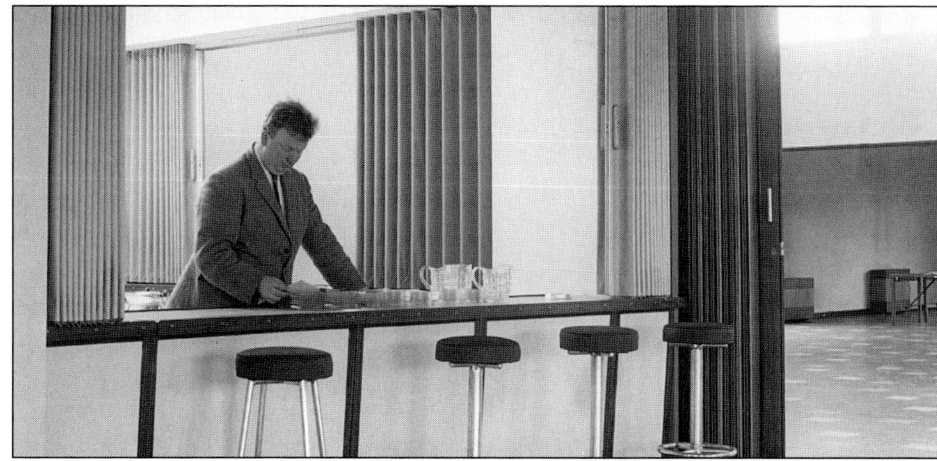

Grantham Youth Centre opened on New Beacon Road in 1964. It included a committee room and reading room with a small library and this coffee bar.

Residents in Harrowby and Cherry Orchard had to queue for water from a 500-gallon tanker when supplies were hit by a cracked water main in 1965. These people are on Harrowby Lane on what appears to be a chilly and windy February day.

Hobart Road, winner of Grantham's best decorated street during the Queen's Silver Jubilee celebrations in 1977.

Members of Grantham 8th (Harrowby) Scouts in 1972 admire a model of the new scout hut planned to be built at the rear of Tennyson Avenue.

A royal wedding street party held in Ermine Close in 1981.

A royal wedding street party held in Hamilton Road in 1981.

Thoroughfares

St Peter's Hill

Youngsters gathered on St Peter's Hill in February 1952 to hear the Proclamation that King George VI was dead and Queen Elizabeth II was the new monarch. Most children then wore short trousers and few men would venture out bare-headed.

The RAF received the Freedom of the Borough of Grantham in July 1952. Amazingly, St Peter's Hill at first look appears to have hardly changed. Closer scrutiny shows a great deal has altered.

The civic parade on Mayor's Sunday in May 1957. The Red Cross contingent is marching along St Peter's Hill, showing how much it has changed in half a century. The Granada and Picture House cinemas are both now long gone, and the International Stores, the Railway Tavern, photographer John MacKay and the Rainbow Café, a milk bar where girls in flared skirts met boys in drainpipe trousers, have also been consigned to history.

Teenagers on a march through town in 1961, protesting at the George Hotel management's decision to try to get rock 'n' roll banned at the Westgate Hall. They are pictured on St Peter's Hill. The building behind them was demolished to make way for a JobCentre.

The Nativity scene at St Peter's Hill became an annual fixture after it was introduced in 1963. Then it was open to the public but as the years rolled by it had to be locked in a secure cage to deter vandals and thieves.

The Procession of Witness on St Peter's Hill in 1972. In the background the dreadful architecture of Tesco and Boots has replaced better, older buildings. The Rainbow Café has given way to the Currys store, although John Hall's furniture shop still remained.

Painters put the finishing touches to the new JobCentre on St Peter's Hill in 1975.

Father Christmas in a stagecoach visiting the Co-op. Upstairs was where they held the annual toy fair. The store became a pub, the Tollemache Inn. Note the stagecoach in 1976 has come from the road junction, now closed to this stretch of road.

Grantham had two Lloyds TSB Banks when this picture was taken in 2000. It was caused by the merger of the two banks. Lloyds, nearest, was purpose-built in the early 1900s, while the TSB moved from Finkin Street in the 1980s, taking over John Hall's furniture shop. The building had previously been a school for the daughters of gentlefolk.

Ever wondered what is behind the shop fronts on St Peter's Hill? This picture taken from the top of the Guildhall in May 2001 shows you.

The King's School Combined Cadet Force, led by Captain Vincent Wells, who was also art master. The picture shows the north side of St Peter's Hill in 1959.

St Peter's Hill in 1934 when parking was already a problem. The street lighting was still by gas and both the green and Newton's statue were protected by railings.

High Street

Coronation Day 1911. High Street has changed greatly since Edward VII sat on the throne. The Coronation was screened later that night at the new Central Cinema. Sharpley's shop in the background was demolished in the 1940s to allow High Street to go straight down Watergate.

The *Journal* offices on the left, behind the bus stop, in a highly decorated High Street for the Queen's Coronation in June 1953. Next door was butcher's Dewhurst. Near the front of the picture is printers and stationers W.G. Harrison, which later moved to the corner of Finkin Street.

Unfortunately the Coronation Day parade negatives of 1953 were destroyed in a flood at the *Journal* but luckily those of Mayor's Sunday, a few days later, survive. Mayor Alderman Joseph Hardacre led the parade to St Wulfram's Church for Mayor's Sunday in 1953, while the Coronation Street decorations were still up. The Mayoral procession turns into Vine Street from High Street. Most of the buildings are familiar 60 years later although their uses and occupants have changed. Burtons became a sports shop and more recently, a substance abuse drop-in centre.

Joseph Hardacre was Mayor at this parade to St Wulfram's Church in 1953. The party, led by macebearers and the Mayor with town clerk John F. Guille, passes the Scotch Wool and Hosiery Stores, next door to the Central Cinema, on one side and Timothy White and Taylors on the other. The cinema had movable seats so the building could also be used as a corn exchange.

Civic dignitaries march past the end of Guildhall Street. Outfitters Foster Brothers was later incorporated into Barclays Bank, which in turn became the Goose at the Bank pub. Hiltons and Johnsons were part of the elegant Waterloo House, which was attached to the George Hotel. It was demolished to make way for a more efficient if less aesthetically pleasing block of shops. The event was Mayor's Sunday 1953, just days after the Coronation celebrations.

Comedian Benny Hill visited Grantham in 1957 and High Street was lined with fans. He was there to promote Alice M. Griffin's hair salon. This picture shows the east side with crowds not only on the pavements but peering from windows. To help anyone who still cannot locate it, Middleton's became Michael Reed, W.H. Smith and later Adams Childrenswear.

The Midland Bank, High Street, in 1932. The following year it was pulled down, together with Fosters tobacconists, to make way for a new Marks & Spencer store which promised nothing would cost more than five shillings (25p). During demolition, an ancient wall some 2m thick and believed to be 600 years old was discovered. It was knocked down and used as hardcore.

Sixth Battalion Lincolnshire Regiment marching along High Street in 1946. Behind them are, from left: furnishers John Hall (later Lloyds TSB bank), Hall's wine merchants and the stone Horse and Jockey pub – pulled down for a new building occupied by Boots – and a pair of buildings which became North's paper shop and later Carphone Warehouse and Goldings. On the right is pharmacists Calverts.

This is the north end of High Street in 1933. Sharpley's was knocked down in the late 1940s to widen Watergate.

A lorry overturned on Grantham High Street spilling its load of rags in 1973. It was left at a precarious angle for firemen trying to make it safe.

Labour leader Michael Foot heads the March for Jobs in November 1981. The George was still a hotel then and the rounded corner shop on Finkin Street was stationers W.G. Harrison. For many years this distinctive High Street corner shop was a stationers, first Nightingales, then Harrisons who moved from the St Peter's Hill end. The premises became a charity shop in 1986.

Big changes were due in Grantham in 1983 when the future of Waterloo House was put in doubt. The George was still a hotel then, too.

Bradley's almshouses, which stood opposite the *Journal's* High Street offices. Up the steps was an unofficial short cut to Elmer Street South. On the left was John Porter's shoe shop and on the right a delightful Georgian building occupied by Mr Wallace, the dentist. All were demolished to make way for a modern, shoebox-like block of shops.

High Street in 1960, with Woolworth's and the new *Journa*l office still under construction. The solid stone building was the Horse and Jockey pub, demolished for what eventually became Boots.

The *Journal*, butchers Dewhurst and O'Brien's cycle shop all came down in 1957 to make way for the new Woolworth's store which incorporated a new *Journal* reception area.

A very busy High Street during the 1986 Grantham Carnival.

London Road

London Road in 1932. On the right is the bus station which had to suffice until the purpose-built one on St Peter's Hill opened the following year.

The Co-op on the corner of London Road and St Catherine's Road looked unimpressive in 1932. After the Co-op closed it became Chicago Rock downstairs with a fitness studio above.

The Railway Queen was escorted along London Road in September 1952. This band was marching past some long-disappeared shops, including the Co-op which became a fitness club, and Boots chemists, which closed in the 1960s when the new High Street branch was completed.

A marching band played along London Road in September 1952 for the Railway Queen's parade. The buildings have changed a little, especially the Welcome Café and the Reindeer Inn, later the Stagger Inn.

North Road Garages moved from Great Ponton where it was formed in the 1920s to the former brewery site, London Road, Grantham, in 1963. It was opened by world motor racing champion Graham Hill, who drove for BRM. Through the window you can see the Windsor fish and chip shop and part of the Blue Horse Inn.

Ian Mann, 13, a Red Cross cadet, had been on duty at Grantham FC's match, London Road, in September 1958. Unfortunately, on his way home, at Wharf Road junction, his cycle collided with a car and although he was unhurt, his bike was beyond repair. On the positive side, it did allow a memorable picture of London Road. This includes, from left, the Co-op, Boots chemists, the Long Bar and Watkin's.

A Triumph Herald was hoisted 30ft on top of North Road Garage's showroom, London Road, in 1967. One of the town's senior dealerships, it began at Great Ponton in 1920. The work was carried out by British Crane and Excavator, whose factory was on Dysart Road. The houses next door were later knocked down to provide a forecourt.

North Road Commercials – a subsidiary of North Road Garages – was one of the first companies to move on to the site vacated by Ruston & Hornsby. The building next door was built as Hornsby's works fire brigade. In the background are the fitting shops known as 'Top End'. These were eventually replaced by Jackson Building Supplies.

Crowds line London Road in 1978 to watch the Barford's Gala parade. The Nag's Head closed and although it had a new lease of life as a restaurant, the units next door remained empty for many years and in 2004 were demolished.

London Road football ground in 1988, before the wall was pulled down to make way for a Safeway supermarket.

Market Place

A huge crowd turned out in Grantham Market Place in 1951 to see Clement Atlee, the first serving Prime Minister to visit the town officially. The buildings have scarcely changed, apart from the names over the fronts.

The buildings are similar but ladies' clothiers Hill and Co. has long gone. The picture was taken in the Market Place at the Proclamation 'The King is Dead – God Save the Queen' in February 1952.

A large crowd gathered to turn the clock back in the Market Place in June 1972. They were there to see the first stagecoach on the London-Edinburgh run for 127 years. It changed its team of horses in Grantham. The background has changed little, except the Royal Oak sold Shipstone's beer and Hill's dress shop has acquired a pointed middle gable.

More youngsters gather to hear the 'King is Dead' Proclamation by the Mayor, Ald William Goodliff, in February 1952. Behind the Grange building was seed merchants Sharpe's, later to become a pub. Marsden and Pearks were both provisions stores, the forerunners of supermarkets.

American TV cameras were in town to record Labour campaigner Woodrow Wyatt at the 1955 General Election. The flamboyant Labour man lost by 2,375 votes to Conservative Joe Godber. Wyatt later became a staunch Tory and devout Thatcherite. In the background is Sharpe's, the seed company, which saw its demise when garden centres opened. Easiephit was a shoe shop.

Stonemasons were called to the Market Cross in 1966 after it was reported to be 'swaying in the wind'. The buildings behind the Market Cross are the same but the labels over the windows have changed. Even the mobile canteen was there.

The Procession of Witness on Good Friday 1995 in the Market Place. Homecare closed soon afterwards to become the Hogshead.

Westgate

Butch the dog waited patiently outside butcher F.J. Woods' Westgate shop every morning for a tit-bit in 1967. The dog, owned by Rex Cummins, who had a Market Place business, would then trot across the road to seed merchants Ogden's for biscuits. Next door was Lyne (Printers).

An unusual view of Wide Westgate taken from the big wheel at the Mid-Lent Fair in 1969. The cottages on the left were demolished to make way for Great Northern Court, while the single-storey building and gate (bottom left) was Pattinson's builder's merchants. The company used the old maltings as a warehouse. The taller building adjacent was variously the Blue Anchor pub, Melton Farmers and Plamore Sport.

FISH&CHIPS
CAPSTAN
XTL 512

A busy Wide Westgate in June 1964, with a fun fair as well as the usual Saturday market. The crowd milling about on the left are probably looking at the lots for the weekly auction of bric-a-brac. The youngsters in the back of the Mini pick-up with the tailgate down would be frowned upon in later times.

Bread queues formed outside private bakeries when the national bakeries went on strike. This is Websters in Westgate.

The Bridge Hotel, which in its later days was Vacu-lug Social Club, was ready for demolition. The site was finally used as the access into Sankt Augustin Way from Wharf Road roundabout. The small house next door marks the end of Westgate Cottages.

Street scenes from the October Criteriums run by Witham Wheelers, Rothwell Racing and Cherry Valley in 1980. The finishing line was outside newsagent's and post office Fosters, Westgate. The buildings were incorporated into the George Centre in the 1990s.

Westgate Cottages in 1981 before they were demolished.

Prime Minister Harold Macmillan visited Grantham in 1959 to support local Conservative MP Joe Godber. The huge crowd blocked Wide Westgate. Across the road was the Blue Man, later the Maltshovel (far left), with traffic coming out of Welby Street. Johnson and Basker was an off-licence, while Manterfield was a cobbler.

Street scenes from the October 1980 Criteriums (cycle races) run by Witham Wheelers, Rothwell Racing and Cherry Valley. The race comes out of Welby Street at a time when it was a through road.

Barrowby Road

A parade by St Mary's Roman Catholic Church celebrating May Day in 1951, led by May Queen Ann Murphy. The sign over the building, the former Catholic School, still said ARP Centre. It later became the Hugh More Club.

Evelyn Annable's car outside her home in Barrowby Road following a collision with another car in February 1952. She was a teacher at the National School. Luckily, she suffered only a bruised knee and shoulder.

Barrowby Road railway bridge was replaced in 30 hours in 1955 and was described as the most delicate structural engineering job the town had seen. The contract, which cost £10,000, began with the railway lines being torn up and the old bridge being cut and removed by two giant cranes. The cranes were soon lifting replacement steelwork into place. The Grantham-Nottingham road was closed for 12 hours while trains were either diverted or halted at Nottingham where passengers continued their journeys by bus.

Looking up Barrowby Road in 1996 before Asda was built and Sankt Augustin Way was still a dream. It was hoped the new road would relieve traffic chaos at the North Parade junction. In the background is Volvo dealers Witham Garage.

That age-old Grantham tradition, a high loaded lorry which thought it could get under Barrowby Road bridge.

Vine Street

Grantham Police march down Vine Street on Battle of Britain Sunday in September 1952. Most of the buildings remain, except the furniture shop in the background, at right angles to Vine House. This was demolished to make way for the Watergate House development.

The Civic parade on Mayor's Sunday, May 1957, returning from St Wulfram's Church along Vine Street. The building behind them, the Cross Swords pub, was pulled down to make way for a store.

The Civic parade on Mayor's Sunday in May 1957. Red Cross cadets reach Vine House. Rudd's furniture shop onwards were demolished to make way for Watergate House and the widening of Watergate.

Elmer Street/ Swinegate

The old chapel, Swinegate, had to go in 1952 to make way for the Empire Garage, Brook Street. The building had a chequered history, having been a Wesleyan chapel, a theatre, gymnasium, saleroom, meeting room and billiard hall. Towards the end of its life it was a warehouse for a vegetable wholesaler.

This lorry driver, heading along High Street, had been told the road for Lincoln was the next right turn. Unfortunately the directions were given by someone in 1987 who forgot about Vine Street. And to add to the driver's woes, his engine failed and a mechanic had to be called when he broke down in Swinegate.

The bottom of Swinegate in 1986, with Donray cycles (owned by Don Ray). A. & A. Glass next door has been there many years, although Barnes TV shop has been replaced.

Youngsters were joined by councillors on a march through town in 1961. They were protesting at the George Hotel management's decision to try to get rock 'n' roll dances banned at the Westgate Hall. Led by Councillor John Wallwork, Alderman Sarah Barnes (centre) and Councillor Elsie Davies, the procession has reached Elmer Street South. Many of the buildings have since been demolished.

Elmer Street North is more open, following the demolition of buildings, since this picture was taken in 1976.

Brook Street

St Wulfram's vicarage still had the Victorian wings in 1956. These were removed shortly afterwards to expose a delightful Georgian building. The garden at the rear, running to Brook Street, has since been built on. On the left is what became Empire Garage and remained a filling station until 2003. The picture was taken from the olliers, the walkway at the top of the church tower.

Harry Watson, of Barrowby, and T.J. Hobb, of Stoke Rochford, with their Ford Classic prepared by Empire Garage, Brook Street, in 1963. Behind them is a street scene that has changed very little.

King's School pupils clearing snow for the pensioners living in Dawson's Almshouses, Brook Street, in February 1991.

That well-known Grantham tradition of always having a main road being excavated. This is Brook Street in February 1996.

St Catherine's Road

It's not every day you see elephants walking down St Catherine's Road – which in those days was lined with houses, not offices. The sight certainly seemed to baffle these shoppers who were expecting a bus. The animals belonged to Sir Robert Fossett's Circus and had arrived by train. They were marching towards Wyndham Park.

This elephant from Sir Robert Fossett's Circus could easily distract from what an interesting photograph this is, taken in a very residential St Catherine's Road in 1957. The double decker is turning into what was then the bus station. It carries a Brewmaster advertisement, a popular drink made by Grantham brewery Flowers. Note also the style of the boy's bike on the right, the butcher-boy bikes coming down the hill and that all small boys wore ties and short trousers.

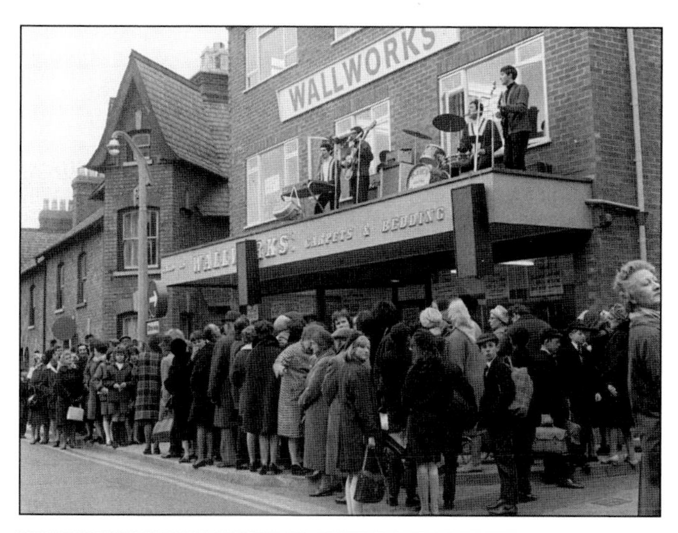

Castlegate

A local band plays to the crowd in April 1966 for the opening of John Wallwork's new furniture showroom in Castlegate. Peter Wallwork is on keyboards. Doing the honours was popular singer Frankie Vaughan.

About 350 people came by bus from Boston to visit John Wallwork's furniture store in Castlegate at Christmas 1972. The local businessman had begun in a small, stone-built secondhand shop on the site of the shop far right. By the 1970s he had built quite a large complex which became variously Status, Fine Fare, Food Giant and Kwik Save.

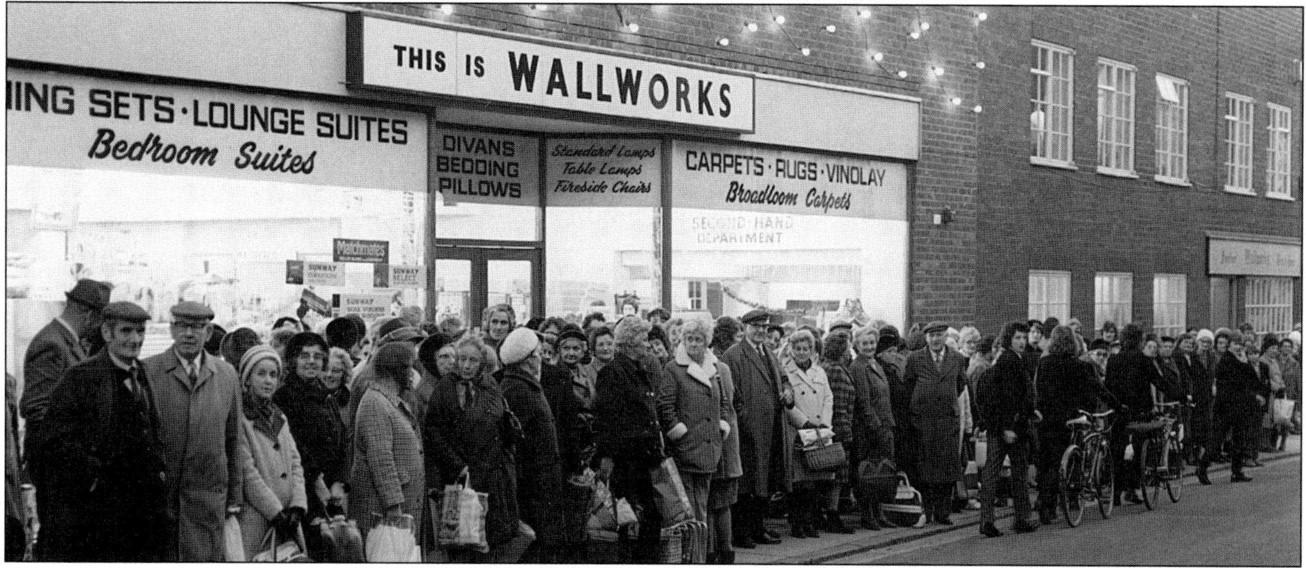

Belton Lane

A parade of Scouts and Cubs crossing Belton Lane bridge across the Witham, long before traffic lights were installed. They were on their way to Wyndham Park in 1953. Together with Guides and Brownies there were about 500 of them.

Steel girders are in place together with timber planks before concrete is poured over to rebuild the bridge over the River Witham at Belton Lane in 1976.

Somerby Hill

A row of cottages stood by the gates of RAF Spitalgate until 1958. They were Somerby Hill Cottages and were a century old when they were demolished. During demolition, a 97ft well was discovered, and it took the rubble from four of the cottages to fill it.

The gatehouse at RAF Spitalgate in 1973. The station had been home to the WRAF and RAF Police but was soon to become an Army barracks.

A lorry loaded with grain travelling down Somerby Hill collided with an electric lamp standard near the bottom in September 1961. No one was hurt. Notice there is no filling station across the road, just allotments.

Grantham Tractor Company, an art deco building at the bottom of Somerby Hill, was demolished in favour of a housing development.

Watergate and North Street

A pair of traction engines wind their way up Watergate in 1934, towing a steel barge. All of the buildings in the picture were demolished in the 1940s for what became Watergate car park.

A lorry squeezes out of Watergate and into High Street carrying a ship's propeller in 1932. Sharpley's shop on the right was demolished 15 years later to widen the road.

A murky day in 1934. Sharpley's shop is on the left and once past the traffic light you are in High Street. The shop on the right sticking out was soon to be demolished and an art deco Burton tailoring building erected in its place.

The buildings on the right at the bottom of Watergate were demolished to make way for Key Markets supermarket while many on the left were sacrificed for a car park. The poster above Hare's shop on the left for Poacher referred to a brown ale made by local brewer Flowers. It would have cost about 10d (4p) a bottle then and was probably the first beer Grantham schoolboys tasted. This St George's Day scout parade was in 1953.

An ambulance was badly damaged in 1955 following a collision with a lorry in Watergate. The lorry was carrying paper. No one was hurt. But it is not the accident which makes the photograph interesting so much as the buildings which were pulled down to build Key Markets superstore (later Gateway and Lidl). Harrisons began as an osier company although when this picture was taken, it also sold toys, prams and suitcases. Even the Co-op was bulldozed for the development.

The Corpus Christi procession of St Mary the Immaculate Church in June 1957. The building on the left remains, although those on the right were demolished as part of a road widening scheme and to create Watergate car park. The girls are coming from Brook Street. The Brewmaster hoarding is for an Indian pale ale produced by Flowers brewery which had taken over Grantham brewers Mowbray.

The face of Watergate changed forever in February 1960 as bulldozers moved in to widen the road and make way for a modern development. Sharpley's had already fallen to widen Watergate.

Watergate House was the flagship in the Watergate redevelopment in 1963. The road at the Vine Street junction was transformed from an old-fashioned bottleneck into a modern building with a much wider road. The picture also shows how Harrison's building caused the road to narrow in the distance and it became a casualty in further road widening.

Work continued on Watergate House in 1964. Demolition also continued on Watergate, but apart from Watergate House (right) nothing else went on the site. First it was used as a temporary car park – then a permanent one.

The old pie shop in North Street was one of the casualties making way for new developments in 1978. Next door is motor dealers R.M. Wright. Blue Lion Lane was later called Union Street, after the workhouse, although the frontage of the shop is in North Street.

Travellers moved on to the vacant plot at the bottom of Watergate in 1985. This had once been the site of Vere Street and James Street. Two pubs, the Sun Inn and the Square and Compass, also came down. Eventually, Premier Court was built on the land.

Islands were installed at Brook Street junction with Watergate in 1996. In the background is the newly-built Premier Court.

Station Road

A party of Scouts march up Station Road (East) wearing their 'lemon squeezer' hats and shorts. The building on the right was part of Ruston and Hornsby's engineering works while the hoardings in the background disguise London Road sports ground.

The water tower in Station Road West in 1985.

Springfield Road

Springfield Road allotments. In 1972 these were earmarked for Grantham FC's new stadium but 30 years later the gardeners were still there, even though they had to reinforce the fencing to keep out vandals.

The bridge over Springfield Road, which for more than a century had linked Ruston and Hornsby's London Road works with 'Top End' on South Parade, was taken down in 1982. It had been redundant for more than a decade since the factory closed. Unfortunately for heavy traffic, the railway bridge further along remained.

St John's Church Hall, on the corner of Springfield Road and Stamford Street, was demolished to make way for housing in 1977. Its bowling green was believed to have once been the town's only crown green. The houses were known as The Lindens. Ruston and Hornsby's Top End can just be seen across the railway line, through the poplars.

Three women and two toddlers were injured when a scrap car fell from a trailer in April 1980, trapping them against a wall in Springfield Road. They were rescued by passers-by and draymen unloading barrels at the Springfield Arms opposite. The shop opposite Huntingtower Road closed in the 1990s and became a private house.

Avenue Road, Stonebridge Road and Welham Street

The south side of Avenue Road in 1953 with Dr Charles Frier (centre) wishing under-privileged children good luck as they set off for Skegness. The trips were paid for by Dr Frier's Children's Holiday Fund, which continues to this day.

Mayor Ernest Hardy and borough engineer J. Livesby inspect new benches in the paddock, also known as Stonebridge Close, off Avenue Road, in 1953. They were paid for out of surplus Coronation funds from Grantham's Spittlegate ward. The field was given to the town at the end of the war by owner Mrs Schwind on condition nothing is built on it.

The snow was deep and crisp and even in Avenue Road (now Stonebridge Road) in January 1958. On the left is the police station and on the right is Kesteven and Grantham Girls' School. Further down you can just see the entrance to Grantham College.

The driver of this precariously balanced Mini was unhurt following a collision on the corner of Welham Street and Avenue Road in 1959. In the background is Pidcock's Maltings, which was demolished in 1973.

Demolition of Pidcock's Maltings in 1973. The Victorian building, which ran the length of Welham Street North, was probably built in about 1865. The site was later used for sheltered housing.

Students from Kesteven Teacher Training College, Stoke Rochford, marching up Avenue Road to a grants protest at the Guildhall in 1974. Welham Street maltings have gone but the lodge at the bottom of Grantham College for Further Education (as it was then) is still there.

The Fireworks 5 children's race in Welham Street. Pidcock's maltings has been demolished but the new Riverside complex has yet to be built. Early in the 19th century the Queen's Mill and ducking stool had stood at the north end of Welham Street.

Wharf Road and Old Wharf Road

Wharf Road in 1906. A lifeboat makes its way to the Grantham Canal bound for Skegness. It was paid for by public subscription. The house nearest the camera was demolished in the early 1980s to make way for the Isaac Newton Centre. The next building is the Baptist church before it was remodelled.

Employee Syd Duller surveys the demolition work at builders' merchants English Bros depot in 1970. It had been Premier Rinks and its origins were exposed when English Bros (later Jewsons) brought in the demolition men to their Wharf Road depot in 1970. The building began as Richard John Boyall's carriage and tram works, later becoming the orderly room for the 2nd Battalion Lincolnshire Regiment. By the 1880s it was the Premier Skating Rink and later doubled as the King's Picture Hall, a cinema seating 800. By 1918, it was home to the YMCA before returning to commercial use.

Wharf Road changed almost entirely in 1984, not least because of the town's first multi-storey car park.

Wharf Road in 1986. It has changed little on the south side apart from the business names and a distinct lack of traffic.

Derelict maltings on Wharf Road were ear-marked as a theatre in 1986. Previously, they were a store for a builders' merchants. The building had been hidden behind Jackson's Garage for many years.

Old Wharf Road steel warehouses in 2001.

The site of the former Wesleyan School in Wharf Road. In 1994, it was being used as a car sales plot and was later developed for flats.

Wharf Road roundabout in 1996 before Sankt Augustin Way was linked to it.

Wharf Road roundabout five years later, with the Sankt Augustin Way link. The roundabout became a motorist's nightmare.

Wharf Road seen from the multi-storey car park in 1997. The John Smith pub was then known as Warthogs – nickname of landlord Tony Willows – having previously been the Golden Fleece. Latterly, it became Churchills.

John Lee and Son, of Old Wharf Road, completing an order for 100,000 jute sacks destined for Louisville, Kentucky, in 1971. Most of the buildings have since been demolished.

Spittlegate Hill and South Parade

Members of Kesteven County Council planning committee paid a visit to Spittlegate Hill in 1966 to see the proposed caravan site for gypsies, later known as Travellers' Rest. At the time, the preferred site was Alma Park.

Six months of traffic chaos was the prospect in 1972 as Spittlegate Hill bridge over the London-Edinburgh railway line was demolished and rebuilt, costing £98,000, a lot of money in those days. The diversion on the left was down Albert Street. Wyville Road was resurfaced as an alternative route for light vehicles making for the A1.

Broad Street

The ice cream van driver had a lucky escape on the Broad Street/North Street junction when his vehicle collided with a lorry load of bananas in June 1955. J.F. Flint's butchers shop in Broad Street has long been demolished. His windows always displayed pigs' heads with an apple stuffed in their mouths. Across the road was Hopkin's Garage with roadside petrol pumps. It eventually became R.M. Wright.

The Corpus Christi procession of St Mary the Immaculate Church in June 1957. The parade is moving down Broad Street. The shop on the far corner is the birthplace of Prime Minister Margaret Thatcher. The houses next door have been demolished.

Mayor Ernest Smith was Roman Catholic so for the first time the service was held at St Mary's Church. He is in the centre, behind the mace-bearers, flanked by deputy Mayor Tom Smith and the town clerk. This picture was taken outside the church, showing Peacock's butchers, formerly J.F. Flint, on the corner of North Street and Broad Street. All the buildings in the background were demolished and eventually became Premier Court.

North Parade

May Queen Margaret Cassidy, aged seven, at St Mary's Church, North Parade, in 1955. About 150 children aged five to 15 took part in the ceremony where the statue of Our Lady was crowned. The houses opposite appear lacklustre and some of the skylights have been boarded up although little else has changed.

The Corpus Christi procession of St Mary the Immaculate Church traditionally confined itself to the church. In June 1957 it was decided to take it to the streets. This is North Parade, with prams lined up outside the church.

The most famous corner shop in Britain, where Britain's first woman Prime Minister Margaret Thatcher was born. The picture was taken in 1975 on the corner of North Parade and Broad Street. The corner shop belonged to Alderman Alfred Roberts, father of the former Prime Minister. She lived there until she left Kesteven and Grantham Girls' School for university, fame and fortune. The shop became first a restaurant, then a chiropractic centre.

Roberts shop, North Parade, birthplace of Prime Minister Margaret Thatcher, became a target for anti-unemployment protesters in 1981.

Finkin Street

Members of Grantham Old Contemptibles marching down Finkin Street in 1961. On the far corner is sports shop Wilkinson and Hawley, next door to Grantham Waterworks. The building with the arches was the tax office. In the background, the George was then a thriving hotel.

Finkin Street was blocked to traffic by a large crowd which assembled in April 1966 for the opening of John Wallwork's new furniture showroom, Castlegate, by singer Frankie Vaughan. The building to the right began life as Brownlow School – later Girls' Central School – and became a printer's workshop and later a land agent.

Albion Place

A 12-ton coal lorry's brakes failed on Barrowby Road hill. It careered into a house in Albion Place, ironically owned by retired coal merchant J.W. Storey.

The Catholic processions produced a number of pictures in streets which would otherwise be ignored. This one celebrated the Feast of Corpus Christi in 1960 with a march which took them down Albion Terrace.

Harrowby Road

There are not many car tracks in the snow as these cyclists tackle the harsh weather of January 1958. The Barracks is unchanged, other than there are noticeboards outside, showing which top group would perform there next. John Dankworth, Ted Heath, the Who, the Walker Brothers and Cream are among many top bands who appeared there. Note also the school sign.

A snow-covered road welcomed Father Christmas when he visited New Somerby Institute, Harrowby Road, for a Christmas party for the children of employees at Grantham Motor Company. Sixty children were there.

Union Street

Grange flats are in the background of this picture of Union Street in 1974. The car park was for the leisure centre.

Many – but not all – of the old outbuildings off Union Street seen here in 1985 were demolished during redevelopment of the area.

Grange Gardens being built off Union Street in 1959. They would provide homes for 27 families and cost £37,000 using new Unity pre-cast methods.

Alma Park

A strike at Superfoam, Alma Park, caused by the sacking of a shop steward, brought out the pickets in 1972. The company refused to speak with the union and the dispute dragged on.

Poachers Motor Club found Wyndham Park too wet for their rally in 1960, so they moved to the former RAF Regiment parade ground at Alma Park. The buildings were used as starter homes for people moving on to council houses. They were later pulled down to make way for an industrial estate.

Launder Terrace and Commercial Road

The Mayor and Mayoress, Coun. and Mrs Ernest Hardy, inspect the Girl Guides in front of St John's Church, Spittlegate, on St George's Day, 1955. Many of the Launder Terrace houses in the background have gone.

Mayor of Grantham Coun. Montague Ogden and his daughter-in-law arriving at St John's Church, Spittlegate, in 1967 for the St George's Day service. In the background, mainly Commercial Road, are many buildings which have since disappeared. One of them is Lee and Grinling's Commercial Road maltings. On the side of the building it states Church Terrace, although most people consider this short-cut from London Road to the railway station as Nursery Path.

The Dolphin Inn was a casualty when Victorian buildings were pulled down in 1970 to make way for a new three-storey development of 18 flats on Commercial Road. This was the first photograph taken for the *Journal* by Gerald Wright from the tower of St John's Church. Many of the buildings on the right nearest the camera were later demolished.

The Maltings Dental Practice, Commercial Road, originally opened in 1979, was fully restored by October 1981.

Park Lane

Mayor Ernest Smith used to turn up in the most unlikely places. Here he is in Park Road. The buildings behind him made way for a filling station on Manthorpe Road. He is with borough engineers inspecting the culvert which took the Mowbeck under Brook Street until it discharged in the River Witham near the White Bridge in Wyndham Park.

Harlaxton Road

Harlaxton Road bridge with a double decker stuck beneath. This is one of five railway bridges in the town frequently hit by high vehicles.

A Mini and a Ford Cortina collided on Harlaxton Road in 1980, conveniently outside the fire station. The buildings in the centre were a county council depot before they became home to a motor dealership.

The Parkinson family took daughter Louise for a ride along Harlaxton Road's snow-covered pavements in 1985.

Builders' merchants and roofing contractors Arthur Syddall's offices on Harlaxton Road were demolished in 1995 to make way for a car wash.

A traffic jam on Harlaxton Road in May 1997.

Welby Street and Greenwoods Row

A motorcycle caught fire in Welby Street in 1972. No one was hurt but it gave the *Journal* photographer a rare excuse to show how Welby Street looked before the bulldozers moved in.

Greenwoods Row after the marquees hosting the 1974 Grantham Trades Fair were blown down in a gale. The houses in the background are Welby Street. At the time this road from Welby Street was the entrance to Greenwoods Row car park before the Isaac Newton Centre development. Welby Street then linked Wide Westgate with Wharf Road.

Welby Street, still a road in 1986, but only as far as the Isaac Newton Centre.

Welby Street pedestrianisation was completed in September 1991.

Guildhall Street

Guildhall Street was an even tighter squeeze in 1976 when Barclays Bank decided to extend the first floor over the pavement. It would be even worse later when Waterloo House (left) was demolished.

Guildhall Street in 1976 before the Guildhall Car Company (previously Campion Depot) was demolished. The company moved to London Road. The wall on the left was demolished, but the former Guinness bottling plant was converted into shops.

Blue Court, which had four outdoor privies for the eight houses, was ready to be knocked down in 1977. Fortunately, the main block was saved and converted into a small, prestigious group of shops.

Dysart Road

Dysart Road railway bridge (the private one) was closed for repairs in 1971 after a container lorry struck it, causing cracks in two places. The view towards town shows the John Lee Steel (later Corus) warehouse.

The view from the private railway bridge on Dysart Road in 1971. The white buildings belong to Chandler's Fuels with the Coles Crane factory in the background.

Manthorpe Road

Grantham Auto Supplies, Manthorpe Road, in 1971. Originally a corner shop and birthplace of Dr William Wand, Bishop of London. It later became a Chinese supermarket, then after becoming derelict was demolished to extend the filling station.

Traffic lights were installed at the junction of Manthorpe Road and Belton Lane as a first phase in traffic improvements in 1971. It is hard to imagine a signal-free junction any more.

Bridge End Road

Workmen clear up after a 16-wheel Mercedes coke lorry was involved in a fatal collision on the corner of South Parade and Bridge End Road in 1966. The vehicle careered into Muriel Redmile's antiques shop, which was demolished. Behind is Lee and Grinling's maltings, which was due for demolition at the time. On the right is Alfred Wiseman's (previously Ruston and Hornsby's) 'Top End' factory.

The 1,400-mile Tour of Britain cycle race clipped through town in 1964, turning here from South Parade into Bridge End Road on the Oakham to Cleethorpes stage. On the left is the antiques shop, later destroyed by a lorry, and to the right is the Manners Arms pub and filling station.

The Wesleyan Church, Bridge End Road, was demolished in 1966. It had been shut since 1964. The church began in a cottage in Inner Street and moved to Bridge End Road in 1875, to land donated by industrialist William Hornsby. The tower, church and cottages came down leaving only the old schoolroom which was converted into a nightclub and a large car park. The shop also survived. On the extreme left is Lee and Grinling's maltings.

Gainsborough Corner filling station opened in May 1969. It was run by the Grantham Motor Company. It replaced Lee and Grinling maltings and Mrs Redmile's antiques shop.

A lorry carrying a 65ft long concrete beam crashed into one of Mill Cottages on the north side of Bridge End Road, close to the river bridge, in 1967. Fortunately, the couple who lived there were about to move and were given the key to their new home a few days early.

The end of the line for the Bridge End Road maltings in January 1969, making way for Gainsborough Corner filling station. It was previously owned by Joe Thompson and was bought by Lee and Grinling in 1930. It was a floor malting for drying barley prior to malting. At one time there were dozens of maltings in Grantham but by the turn of the 21st century only one was used for its original purpose.

Vere Court

Neighbours in Vere Court, off Broad Street, turn out for a street party during the Grantham Borough Council Centenary celebrations in 1935. Although this was the town's poorest area, the residents always made a big effort at times of celebration.

The entrance to Vere Court. The buildings on the left were demolished but the one on the right remains. This road is now merely an access to the rear of properties on North Parade, plus one or two workshops. It hardly seems credible now that so many houses were squeezed on to this site.

One of the back yards of Vere Court with the outdoor privies on the left. A bath hangs on the wall and beneath it the mangle. In the 19th century, before water closets were installed, residents emptied their toilets on to a midden, which was taken away by the night soil men by horse and cart.

Inner Street

Inner Street was an area of sub-standard housing but there was a tremendous camaraderie. Built in the early 19th century, many were one-up one-down, although most had two bedrooms for some very large families. Water was a single tap in the back yard which, like outdoor privies, was shared with the neighbours. This is one of the back yards. Many of the houses were demolished in the late 1930s just after this picture was taken.

A back yard in Inner Street in the 1930s. These houses, even in the 1930s, had no services. Cooking and heating was done on a range and lighting by candle or hurricane lamp.

A firefighter tackles a £50,000 blaze at John Lee's Warehouse, Inner Street, in 1960. The building was 200m long and the scene of the biggest fire in Grantham's living memory. It happened on a Saturday night, as the pubs and dance halls were turning out, and proved to be a big attraction. The building was gutted.

The aftermath of the 1960 blaze at John Lee's Warehouse, Inner Street. Although used as a warehouse for old fabrics, it had originally been built in the early 1800s by Richard Hornsby as a blacksmiths shop. Inner Street became known as The Street Behind the Chimneys because of the giant flues.

Denton Avenue, built in the mid-1950s, in the winter of 1982. Across the middle is Grantham Road Services depot and, behind it, the industrial workshops of Hollis Road. Beyond is Earlesfield estate.

Other Streets

The former Machine Gun Corps Post Office, dating from World War One, on the Hill Avenue-Belton Lane junction. It was demolished in 1974.

The Barracks Square, off Beacon Lane, in 1981. The 21 houses were built by the Army but were by this time owned by the county council.

A royal wedding street party, celebrating the marriage of the Prince of Wales to Lady Diana Spencer, held in Shorwell Close in 1981. On the right is Town Mayor Joe Flatters.

The 40-year-old prefabs in Belton Avenue got a facelift in January 1983. Built just after World War Two as a stop-gap measure, they cost £14,000 each to modernise. A brick skin was built on the outside before the original walls were removed. The picture shows before and after.

The German-made Okal house being built on Barrowby Gate nears completion in 1988. This revolutionary technique failed to catch on. At one stage the building was used as Gifts hospice and later a day nursery.

Sandon Close bungalows opened in 1988, a £1.1 million complex for 72 people on the site of former district council offices, which had been condemned as unsafe.

Terraced houses in Redcross Street in 1994.

Stanton Street seen from the multi-storey car park in 1997. In the distance is the Blue Bull pub.

Victoria Street, off Springfield Road, in 2000.

Witham Place was flooded in March 1975 with front doors sandbagged. The buildings were soon to be pulled down and replaced by sheltered housing. In the background is Bridge End Road.

The 1974 Milk Race, the Tour of Britain cycle race, shoots out of Brownlow Street. Broad Street is in the background, but Premier Court is yet to be built.

Aerial Photographs

RAF Spitalgate from the air in 1956. The road snaking on the left is Somerby Hill with the small market town of Grantham in the background.

This picture is great fun if you read no further but instead try to guess where it is. And yes it is Grantham, honest. Imagine the plane is somewhere over Belton Park Golf Club. In the bottom right is Belton Lane Primary School and the field on the left, surrounded by houses, is Harrowby playing field. The square on the left contains the Church of the Ascension, with Edinburgh Road going upwards. Running left to right is Harrowby Lane, which joins New Beacon Road with a kink at Pensions Corner. Behind is Hall's Hill, looking distinctly flat from the air. And a lot of building has gone on since this photograph was taken in August 1960.

Grantham from the air in September 1960. The area on the right was demolished to make way firstly for the Union Street Leisure Centre, then Asda superstore. The west side of the railway line looks very under-developed compared with 40 years later.

This aerial shot of Wyndham Park (centre) was taken in 1978 and makes the town look very open. The curving road at the bottom is Belton Lane.

Grantham from the air in 1979. The road moving from the bottom left corner is Springfield Road, moving towards the junction with London Road and Bridge End Road. The large square towards the top left is the London Road cricket ground, later Safeway supermarket.

Town centre developments were just beginning when this aerial picture was taken in March 1980. The road snaking through the centre of the picture is Wharf Road, with Jackson's Garage at the bottom, on the junction with Westgate, before there were any thoughts of a roundabout. Rutland Street has been demolished to make way for a future Isaac Newton Centre, while Stanton Street is to be the next victim. Halfway up on the right is the Granada, by then restricted to bingo, while the London Road football/cricket ground is in the top right corner.

Grantham looking southwards from the tower crane above the George shopping centre. In the foreground is Barclays Bank, later to become the Goose at the Bank pub.

Fenland Foods factory (bottom right) from the air in 1988. The houses are off Shaw Road, with Swingbridge Road running parallel (right). Top right is Spitalgate School.

The Isaac Newton shopping centre from the air in 1988. Forming the triangle of roads are High Street (bottom), Watergate (right) and Wharf Road. Across the top is the railway line.

A plane flies over Grantham College in 1995. Running upwards on the left is St Catherine's Road.

Grantham Meres Leisure Centre and South Kesteven Stadium as seen from the air in 2001. Beyond is the Earlesfield estate.

This view of Grantham in 2001 is easy once you get your bearings. The church near centre top is the cemetery chapel. The buildings on the lower right are London Road developments including Currys and B&Q.